My Love

Other books by Lesléa Newman

Novels

Good Enough to Eat
In Every Laugh A Tear
Fat Chance

Short Story Collections

A Letter To Harvey Milk
Secrets
Every Woman's Dream

Poetry Collections

Love Me Like You Mean It
Sweet Dark Places
Still Life with Buddy

Nonfiction

SomeBODY To Love: A Guide to Loving the Body You Have
Writing from the Heart: Inspiration and Exercises for Women Who Want to Write

Humor

Out of the Closet and Nothing to Wear
The Little Butch Book

Anthologies

The Femme Mystique
Pillow Talk: Lesbian Stories Between the Covers

Children's Books

Heather Has Two Mommies
Saturday Is Pattyday
Too Far Away To Touch
Remember That
Matzo Ball Moon

My Lover Is a Woman

Contemporary Lesbian Love Poems

Edited by

Lesléa Newman

Ballantine Books
New York

A Ballantine Book
Published by The Ballantine Publishing Group

 Published in the United States by The Ballantine Publishing Group, a division of Random House, Inc., New York, and simultaneously in Canada by Random House of Canada Limited, Toronto. Originally published in slightly different form by The Ballantine Publishing Group in 1996.

www.randomhouse.com/BB/

Library of Congress Catalog Card Number: 99-90324

ISBN 0-345-42114-0

Manufactured in the United States of America

Cover design by Barbara Leff
Cover painting © Robert Anderson, *Sisters & Secrets II,* 1991

First Hardcover Edition: February 1996
First Trade Paperback Edition: June 1999

10 9 8 7 6 5 4 3 2

dedicated to the one I love:

MARY GRACE VAZQUEZ

Contents

Acknowledgments

I'd like to thank Joanne Wyckoff, editor extraordinaire, and her able assistants, Andrea Schultz and Ann Weinerman, of Ballantine Books; Charlotte Cecil Raymond, my wonderful agent; and my colleagues Tzivia Gover, Joan Larkin, Sharon Lim-Hing, Terri L. Jewell, Paula Neves, Mariana Romo-Carmona, tatiana de le tierra, Kitty Tsui, Shay Youngblood, and Irene Zahava for their support. I also want to thank all the poets who gave me the privilege of reading and considering their work for publication, as well as all the publishers who so generously granted me permission to reprint poems. I am especially grateful to the publishers and estates of the late Audre Lorde, Pat Parker, Muriel Rukeyser, and May Swenson for allowing me to include their work in this collection. A special thank-you goes to the estate of Pat Parker and to Firebrand Books for allowing me to use the line "My lover is a woman" from Pat Parker's poem of the same title from her book of poems, *Movement in Black*, as the title for this collection. Lastly, I am more grateful than words can say to my beloved, Mary Grace Vazquez, for teaching me the meaning of love.

Introduction

How does she love she? Let us count the ways!

When I was invited by an editor at Ballantine Books to edit an anthology of contemporary lesbian love poems, I jumped at the chance to sink my teeth into such a delicious project. Before I even hung up the phone, I had jotted down the titles of several poems I wanted to include in the collection: "First, I want to make you come in my hand," by Marilyn Hacker; "Lover's Wish," by Patricia Donegan; "Sometimes, as a child," by Olga Broumas. After I hung up the phone I made a list of poets whose work I admired and wanted to publish. This list included the names of some of the finest writers of any gender or sexual orientation writing poetry today: Dorothy Allison, Paula Gunn Allen, Cheryl Clarke, Jewelle Gomez, Judy Grahn, Irena Klepfisz, Minnie Bruce Pratt, Margaret Randall, Adrienne Rich, and Ruth L. Schwartz.

In addition, I selected work from well-known lesbian writers such as Melinda Goodman, Terri L. Jewell, Victoria

Lena Manyarrows, Cherríe Moraga, Joan Larkin, Judith McDaniel, Honor Moore, Eileen Myles, Linda Smukler, Kitty Tsui, and Shay Youngblood. I also sent out a call for manuscripts to a variety of publications. These included professional writers' journals such as *Poets & Writers* and *Lambda Book Report*; national lesbian magazines such as *Deneuve* (now called *Curve*); and regional lesbian and gay periodicals such as *Bay Windows* (Boston) and *Bay Area Reporter* (San Francisco). Writers I knew who had previously edited anthologies cautioned me against sending out a call. Why not simply solicit poems from writers whose work I already knew? Certainly that method would have been simpler and much less time-consuming. But even though I had over one hundred poets to contact, and over twice that many poetry books and anthologies to read through, I felt it was important to give as many lesbians as possible the chance to have their voices heard. I am proud of the fact that some extremely talented poets are being published in this anthology for the very first time: Ghazala Anwar, Laura Castellanos del Valle, Lynn Goldfarb, Emily Lloyd, Ann McBreen, Susan V. McGovern, and Jessica Weissman.

How *did* I go about selecting a mere 202 poems from the thousands I read in books, journals, magazines, anthologies, and manuscripts? Emily Dickinson wrote, "If I feel physically as if the top of my head were taken off, I know that is poetry." While the top of my head never actually left the rest of my body, I can say that each poem in *My Lover is a Woman* elicited some type of spontaneous physical response from me the first time I read it. Adele Gorelick's poems, "Sweet Dreams," "My Cynic," and "Visit Me," all written about the loss of her lover to cancer, made me weep; Aryn A. Whitewolf's fantasy, "Bus Stop Lover," made me laugh out loud. Lori Cardona's poem about sexual abuse, "Note to My Lover's Brother," made my fingers curl into a fist of rage; I sighed at the tenderness of Sarah Van Arsdale's "Lullabye"; and my eyes widened at the urgency of Doris L. Harris's "Climb Inside of Me." Of course, the frank and beautiful eroticism of many of the poems made various parts of my body quiver with delight: "AT&T," by V.K. Aruna, "She Loves," by Olga Broumas, "Loving You Has Become a Political Act," by Bonnie Morris, and "Desire," by Deidre Pope. And being a poet myself, the sheer beauty of the language of the following poems made me gasp out loud: "To Praise," by Ellen Bass; "You Ask Me for a Love Name," by Chrystos; "Breath #11" and "Breath #14," by H. Emilia Paredes; "Sailor," by Gerry Gomez Pearlberg; and "the very inside," by Indigo Som.

When I told a male colleague that I had completed *My Lover is a Woman*, his response was one of disbelief: "You mean you found enough lesbian love poems to fill a three-hundred-page book?" As I sputtered an angry reply, he interrupted me. "Of course I know there are a lot of lesbians writing poetry out there, but *good* poetry?" I was not in the least bit surprised at the vast number of high-quality poems I read, far too many to include in merely one volume. I *was* surprised, and pleasantly so, by the variety of the poems. "The Ride," by Karen Jastermsky and "Kissing Coco," by

Liz Queeney address puppy love lesbian-style; "Marriage," by Mary Ann McFadden concerns itself with the ups and downs of a long-term, monogamous relationship. Unrequited love is explored in "Anything," by Ana Marie Castañon and "My Crush on the Yakima Woman," by Janice Gould. Poems about having loved and lost include "Last Kiss" and "Missing You," by Laura Castellanos del Valle and "Black Slip," by Terry Wolverton.

Others themes emerged as well. On the serious side are poems about illness and disability, including "How to Talk to a New Lover about Cerebral Palsy," by Elizabeth Clare and "Two Days Before My Stroke," by Margaret Robison, as well as poems about aging such as "Lesbian Menopause," by Mary Clare Powell. Interracial relationships are looked at in "Differences," by Pamela Gray, a Jewish poet, and in "My lover is a woman," by Pat Parker, a Black poet. The theme of lesbians of color loving each other is celebrated in "We Always Were," by Folisade, "HomeComing," by Willyce Kim, and "Longing," by Margaret Sloan-Hunter.

On the lighter side, the deliciousness of forbidden love is explored in "Married Ladies Have Sex in the Bathroom," by Sally Bellerose and "A Born-Again Wife's First Lesbian Kiss," by Mary Diane Hausman. And the joys of femme-butch sexuality are revealed in "The Butch Speaks," by Amy Edgington and "First of the Motorcycle Poems," by Lori Faulkner. Even the theme of food was not ignored in poems such as "Honeydew Night," by Paula Amann, "Plum Poem," by Chaia Heller, and "eating szechuan eggplant," by Thérèse

Murdza. Clearly, the variety of the experience of lesbian love is no less than the variety of all human experience.

All of the poems in *My Lover is a Woman* are political poems, for writing a poem about two women in love is a political act. Even at the tail end of the twentieth century, lesbians can and do lose our homes, jobs, children, and lives simply by being who we are. To write about our love for one another is an act of courage, defiance, and survival. Still, several poems stand out for their political stance: Denise Nico Leto's poem, "What I Think of When You're Gone," speaks of the fear one woman feels concerning the safety of her butch lover who is away for the weekend:

> . . . It is not
> car accidents or earthquakes I imagine.
> It is violence. That bare and simple.
> Even a short separation:
> a run to the store, a weekend camping
> could take you from me.
> Someone could hate you in just the right amount
> that day . . .

Minnie Bruce Pratt's poem, "To Be Posted on 21st Street, Between Eye and Pennsylvania," tells the story of two lovers who are verbally abused on the street:

> . . . Around the corner screamed
> a car, the men, shouts: *Dykes, dykes*. Have you

ever tried to frighten someone out of their life?
Just having a good time, like shooting at ducks
down by the Bay, or at the office telling jokes.
Nothing personal except to the ones getting hit
other side of the threat . . .

For a woman to love another woman, she has to first love herself, also a profoundly political act that goes against everything American culture teaches us. In "My Next Lover," Becky Birtha states:

My next lover can flirt with whomever she likes.
We'll both know it's not serious.
And while many women will probably want her
my next lover will want to stay with me.
She'll know she'll never get
a better offer.

And, in "A Pacifist Becomes Militant and Declares War," Kate Rushin discovers:

Your sudden
Street corner kiss
Accentuates my hesitation
And I realize that in order to care about you
I have to be everything that is in me . . .

. . . And if I love you
Even just a little bit
I have to love the woman that I am

I have to reach down deep inside
I have to stand and show myself
I have to walk in the world
There is never any going back
Only going into the next day
And the day after that . . .

It is my hope that this collection will help every lesbian who reads it love the woman that she is, and that other readers will come to a better understanding of who we are, and thus join us in celebration of lesbian love.

Lesléa Newman
February 1999

My Lover is a Woman

Donna Allegra

Looking Back

She first thought me
a shadow wrinkling a sunlit field,
a flicker of doubt
in the corner of her eye

I'd lived in this garden
since forever,
had been around in the beginning,
was old as dirt
and running neck-to-neck
with God

though a lady never reveals
her true age, I winked,
simply inviting her
to have a bite

She giggled
glad to join me
in a secret kept
from the old man

So under the leaves
she tasted another miracle
felt clean and fresh in her skin
touched, as if she'd created

her flesh, its limbs
knew herself to be
juicy, crisp and firm—
fresh as an apple

We knew each other
would've been friends for life
forever at peace
in that garden

but the old man's voice
cast a cold shadow
on our sunny afternoon
when he called her name,
Eve.

Pretty in the Dark Morning

She lay pretty in the dark morning
a magic woman, voodooed long lashes
red clay lining the rivers in her face
sweeps in the brown earth under her cheeks

pink and ivory treasures in the cavern
of her mouth
her skin—clear waters
her fuller breast—a cupping handful

a gold-tooth Jamaican woman
when she smiles the sun glitters
cold, tinsels
pretty in the dark morning

a down-home sister
who ain't political or nothing
drinks beer and smokes reefer and likes
potato chips

bubbling with Caribbean sweetness
chunks of mango after codfish
tall, raspberry-dressed
still touching bells in my head

ruby-ripe lips slightly pout
blackberry kisses on taste
eyes sad and far away
eyes like almonds
I want to tongue and swallow whole

She's turning me sweet
and ripe and dripping
and she's so pretty
in the dark morning.

He Na Tye Woman

Water.
Lakes and rivers.
Oceans and streams.
Springs, pools and gullies.
Arroyos, creeks, watersheds.
Pacific. Atlantic. Mediterranean.
Indian. Caribbean. China Sea.
(Lying. Dreaming on shallow shores.)
Arctic. Antarctic. Baltic.
Mississippi. Amazon. Columbia. Nile.
Thames. Sacramento. Snake. (undulant woman river.)
Seine. Rio Grande. Willamette. McKenzie. Ohio.
Hudson. Po. Rhine. Rhône.
Rain. After a lifetime of drought.
That finally cleanses the air.
The soot from our eyes.
The dingy windows of our western home.
The rooftops and branches. The wings of birds.
The new light on a slant. Pouring. Making everything new.

Water (woman) that is the essence of you.
He na tye (woman) that is recognition and remembering.
Gentle. Soft. Sure.
Long shadows of afternoon, growing as the light turns
west toward sleep. Turning with the sun.
(The rest of it is continents and millennia.
How could I have waited so long for completion?)

The water rises around us like the goddess coming home.
(Arisen.) Same trip, all things considered, all times

and visions, all places and spaces taken into account
on that ancient journey, finally returned. The maps, the plans,
the timetables: the carefully guided tours into all manner
of futilities. Manners the last turn in the road: arid irony.

(Lady, why does your love so touch me?
(Lady, why do my hands have strength for you?
(Lady, how could I wander so long without you?

Water in falls, misting and booming on the rocks below.
Tall pines in the mist, the deep carved caves.
Water in rivulets. Gathering speed, drops joining in
    headlong flight.
Unnamed rivers, flowing eternally underground,
    unchanging, unchanged.
Water thundering down long dry arroyos, the ancient
    causeways
of our faith. Drought over, at last. Carrying silt,
bits of broken glass, branches, pebbles, pieces of abandoned
    cars,
parts of lost houses and discarded dreams. Downstream.
Storms of water, and we
deluged
singing
hair plastered to our ecstatic skulls,
waving wild fists at the bolts hurled at us from above
teeth shimmering in the sheets of rain (the sheen)
eyes blinded with the torrents that fall fromthroughover
    them:
Rain. The Rain that makes us new.
That rain is you.
How did I wait so long to drink.

Reason Enough to Love You

The night my mama called—a Thursday night—
which meant, certainly, something was wrong,
you took my hand, sitting there on the bed
not interrupting while she told jokes and
I laughed   and I told jokes   and she laughed,
both of us trying to cry so soft, maybe
the other one could pretend not to hear.
You took my hand and held on tight while
my tears ran down your shoulder and mama
told another joke in my left ear.
You didn't make me explain, just held me
and took away some of the fear of dying.

The day they were shouting my name,
everyone looking at me like I was crazy
or had forgotten somehow to dress right
like all those nightmares from my childhood
you put your hand on my neck and squeezed
stayed close to me   stayed close
and put your fear in another place.

And that morning when I woke up crying
not able to say why, it could have been anything,
any of ten good reasons to just lay back and cry,
you slid over and put your whole body over mine
gently, your hand in my hair, your mouth on my ear,

wrapping silence and love and the muscles of your thighs
all around me   and let me cry   let me cry
like no one ever let me before.

Paula Amann

HONEYDEW NIGHT

It's hot enough to scald a cat.
Come up for honeydew
chilled to perfection
and I bet you won't stay cool
as you scoop the juicy
pulp and let it shimmy
down your expectant throat.
How is it? I will ask.
Hits the spot, you will answer
as we look long and deep
into the green spoon scars
because looking at each other
is just too hot.

COOKERY

My love she speaks in parsley
in garlic and well-simmered marinara
in Mediterranean olive flesh
dark and tangy as freckles.
Goat cheese may crumble unto crackers
as we sip our wine by the sea
but her pie crust will endure
three cross-country flights as she does
smiling and be pressed into service
with blueberry and custard core.

She's not easy on the telephone
but look how the rounds of pink trout
drown in herbal cream sauce and
succulent chunks of red pepper
and just as in the fairy tales
the table is suddenly groaning
with cheesy au gratin potatoes
coriander-flecked carrots and
the challah lies plump and shining
under the double flames.

She could care less where things lie
on the staircase in the cellar
but see how the pita bread wedges
make planetary rings around the platter
and a blaze of paprika marks the center

where baba ghanoush and hummus meet
as thick and spiced as the accent from Haifa
as the cookery of a summer night when
mingling sauces and other ingredients
we bring each other slowly to a boil.

Ghazala Anwar

SONGS TOWARDS YOU

when the yeast of your memories
rises in my breast
i roll out the dough
into thin wafers
to be taken
with milk
from Inana's breast

were the keepers
of my father's house
to find them
they would roll me out
into thin wafers
and feed them to the birds
whose breasts
would rise
in songs
towards you

V.K. Aruna

AT&T

dedicated to all those women in long-distance relationships

Last night, as you flirted with me on the telephone,
I sat, wrapped in lavender mists. Naked under
a flickering candle. Mouthing sweet mischief in your
rapid Indian vowels, you whispered language magic
till I dissolved into silent wetness. Knees flung
wide in heated water, I listened to your homegrown
expressions of subtle seduction, drawing water between
my thighs, my skin settled back against the porcelain
of a recreated womb chamber. And when you paused
to gather a thought, the symphony of ripples from hand
cleaving water rose up to greet you across the wires,
leaving you speechless. And for one long moment,
we shared only silence and the quiet breathing
of two women desiring each other a one-hour
plane ride apart.

Jane Barnes

THE DOOR OF SPRING

For L.

No, it's impossible to stop writing you love poems
and come to bed. How do I know which will burn

and which be lost, destroyed in another time
when you are lost on a muddy road and have
nothing we shared together save this scrap
on which is written No, it's impossible to stop
writing you love poems and come to bed. How . . .

But if I came to bed and made such love to you
that your cries could be heard in the other land,
then when you were lost on a muddy road
and had nothing we'd shared together
you might hear your own joy and believe joy
could rise up again. In that case, it's possible to
stop writing you love poems. I'm coming to bed.

The Wind/Door

For L.

Love, you hide in my breast like Oh!
I remember when I first saw you, I shouted,
said, Look out that window! But I didn't
know you were the window just then.
Didn't know I'd already soared through it.

When we sit in the kitchen at night together,
I can tell you the exact moment when I think
if I never live another minute it won't matter,
I feel such joy. Tonight it was when you stood up
and, folding your napkin, said, Coffee, Love?

UNDERTOW

How can this river flow
and yet be so still
that all the burnished trees
stand upside down in its glass?

Where does the fine thread of the current
hide, winding through deep water,
stirring the silty bed
probing small hollows in the banks

and towing the great weight of water
down towards the bridge
where I stand wondering
if anything at all is moving?

I remember throwing Pooh sticks
from a bridge like this:
they would fall in and wait
turning aimless circles

as if unsure which way to go.
Then, gravely, sedately,
they would float under the bridge
and emerge, as I knew they would

like morning emerging from night,
like dreams lingering into breakfast,
like the inexorable current of my life
carrying me downstream to you.

When We Talked in the Rose Garden

When we talked in the rose garden
our words slid along each other
explored and danced
like skin on skin
and the sounds hung
on the perfumed air
shimmering in the heatwave
heavy in sense
meaning beneath meaning
unfurled like breath
on a frosty morning
and our eyes locked
as they did when first your fingers
slipped inside me
when we talked in the rose garden.

Ellen Bass

To Praise

I want to praise bodies
nerves and synapses
the impulse that travels the spine
        like fish darting

I want to praise the mouth
that warm wet lair where the tongue reclines
and the tongue, roused
    slithering a cool path

I want to praise hands
those architects that create us anew
fingers, cartographers, revealing
    who we can become
and palms, cupped priestesses
    worshiping the long slow curve

I want to praise muscle
and the heart, that flamboyant champion
    with its insistent pelting like
    tropical rain

Hair, the sweep of it
    a breeze

and feet, arch taut
    stretching like cats

I want to praise the face, engraved
like a riverbed; it breaks like morning
    like a piñata

Breasts, cornucopia
nipples that jump up, gleeful
    like a child greeting the day

and clitoris, shimmering
a huge tender pearl
        in that succulent oyster

I want to praise the love cries
sharp, brilliant as ice
and the roar that swells in the lungs
        like an avalanche

I want to praise the gush, the hot
spring thaw of it, the rivers
        wild with it

Bodies, our extravagant bodies

And I want to praise you, how you have
lavished yours
upon mine
        until I want to praise

Holding Hands With Janet after the Accident

The first night you came home
we watched *84 Charing Cross Road* on TV.
I sat in a chair next to your hospital bed
and held your hand—the one
not suspended from a trapeze
not cast past the elbow
in plaster and hooked
finger by finger to an outrigger, a rake

of pink plastic, metal, fishing line
rubber bands, suede slings
to keep your fingers from
seizing to a claw. We sat.
And as we watched this honest story
of friendship without plot or drama
we held hands. Your warm fingers
moving slightly against mine, delicately
your thumb moving over mine
in a soft dry stroking.

From time to time we'd shift our hands
and my fingers caressed yours, like grasses
stirring in a small breeze. Before
the movie was over, you were uncomfortable
and I had to get you pills
and milk to protect you from the pills
and the bedpan and more covers, then
less, and the sling
readjusted and exhausted
you fell asleep.
But before that nighttime ordeal

there was this interlude. It was like
holding hands in adolescence at the movies.
I was aware of every nuance.
But unlike then, there was no
hunger, no wanting. Only

gratitude—a word too grand, too many
syllables, for such a quiet feeling.
It was more like a one-celled creature,
utterly simple, utterly complete.

For Janet, at the New Year

The way I want to love you, the way
I want to be loved is
with such abundance, with
so much willing profusion—
like those tiny blue flowers
that turn a glade into a sky blue lake,
or our stars, brilliance strewn
across the black felt sky like a
child gone wild with glitter and glue.

I want a love that quickens the dead
wood of our hearts, rubbing life into the sticks
with the power of seasons, revealing
brittleness to be only winter
with buds straining against the bark.

Fable

It was early fall. You rowed me
around the pond
in your ancient boat.
Tart apples lay in a bag with the cheese.
I read you a story
about two women who could not stop
touching each other.
Trumpeter swans paddled close
and you tossed hard French bread
at their black beaks. When you got cold
I gave you my jacket, the leather glistened
like a delicate skin
moving through trees.
You let the oars float
in the oarlocks; you let the boat
drift in circles. You let the women
from the story climb
into the boat. I could not
stop staring. Soon their desire
took up so much room we had to throw
the apples overboard. We had to sit cramped
at one end. Finally we just waded in
and hauled the skiff and the women
to the pier. The story got wet.
The pond was a dark wound.
You unlocked the car and touched
my back, a kindness, as if
I'd always been your lover.

Morning Poem

Listen. It's morning. Soon I'll see your hand reach
for my watch, the water will agitate in the kettle,
but listen. Traffic. I want your dreams first. And
to slide my leg beneath yours before the day opens.
Wait. We slept late. You'll be moody, the phone
will ring, someone wanting something. Let me put
my hands in your hair. Who I was last night I would
be again. This is how the future holds me, how de-
pression wakes with us; my body shelters it. Let me
put my head on your breast. I know nothing lasts.
I would try to hold you back, not out of meanness
but fear. Oh my practical, my worldly-wise. You
know how the body falters, falls in on itself. Tell me
that we will never want from each other what we
cannot have. Lie. It's morning.

Sally Bellerose

Married Ladies Have Sex in the Bathroom

We did it everywhere.
We were middle-aged women
with middle-aged husbands
and school-aged boy children.

Mostly in daylight.
Mostly in twenty minutes
or less.
In places so common
they'd never suspect.

Every room of both houses,
the cellar,
the garage,
the neighbors' children's four-foot wading pool.
And then there were the bathrooms,
the bathrooms,
the bathrooms of Fitzwillies,
                    the Girls Club,
                        Caldor's,
                      Shop-Rite,
                      the bushes
in back of the bar at the end of the street.

We did it on my picnic table,
and under her picnic table.
We did it in extremes,
dressed for inclement weather.

Coming, fully clothed,
hats,
scarves,
boots,
and mittens.

Coming, buck-screaming naked,
in the hot dirt,

of some Godforsaken road,
with bugs crawling,
in woods that never gave back
her pink lace panties.

We did it lying flat
on the kitchen floor,
our heads pressing up against the kitchen door.
Our bodies barring our boys' entrance.

We did it seated
in my car, moving,
in her car, in the body shop,
at the airport,
on the plane to Baltimore
while she calmly discussed
Women, War and Peace
with another speaker in the next seat.

In the hot tubs,
even though I hate the hot tubs.
On the stairs outside the hot tubs,
not waiting for the couple inside
to come out.
We did it with phones ringing,
kids screaming,
dogs barking,
tubs overflowing,
and dinner burning in the pot.
We did it with fingers so hot
we thought sure we'd be branded forever.

We did it with bodies so tired,
hearts so heavy,
that doin' it was the last thing
on our minds.
Still, something greedy whispered,
get it while you can girls,
because you never know
if or when
you're gonna get again.

We did it and called it empowerment,
lust,
avarice,
and adultery.
We dared man or nature
to deny that doin' it
was anything but sacred.

We flaunted.
We hid.
Tense and tangled,
sometimes we forgot
when to run, when to taunt.

We stopped.
Caught our breaths, confronted.
Like dogs in heat, we fought.
Our lives uprooted,
recovered to fight,
to blame some more.

In the end
we cared for ourselves
enough to stay
alive, in this world, together.

And a year,
and a year,
and the years go by.
Less and less
we press each other.

Still we love.
But oh the sex.
It's never been the same.
Life on the edge is an addiction.
Honest life is pleasant, better, definitely better,
but so damned tame.

Becky Birtha

My Next Lover

My next lover will have a car
maybe a Mercedes.
She won't expect me to bicycle
anywhere!

If we're going to a family wedding
an awards dinner or
a program in the black community on a

Sunday afternoon
where I'm the keynote speaker—
she'll wear a skirt.

My next lover will love kids.
She might even have one or two
of her own. In any case
she'll be crazy about mine.
She'll be thrilled to babysit
when I have to go out of town
even if it's for a month.

My next lover will have something she's
impassioned about and obsessed with
besides me.
There'll be times when she can't wait to
get back to whatever she's
creating. There'll be whole weekends
when she doesn't care
what I do, and won't even notice
if we haven't made love.

But my next lover will always be
available for me.
Whenever I'm ready
her timing will be perfect.

My next lover will be wild about
communication.
When I ask her what's wrong
she'll come out with more than
two syllables.

My next lover will never give up on us.
She'll believe in couples therapy.
If we reach a point where the whole thing
just isn't working anymore—
she'll change.

My next lover can flirt with whomever she likes.
We'll both know it's not serious.
And while many women will probably want her
my next lover will want to stay with me.
She'll know she'll never get
a better offer.

Eleven Months

If our relationship was a baby
we would be counting its age this way.
It might be walking by now
pulling itself to an awesome
twenty-seven inches and
maybe tottering halfway across a room
before collapsing on its bottom.
There would be plenty of time for mistakes.
It would always manage to get
back on its feet again.

If our relationship was a baby
it would be starting to feed itself
in a messy sort of way
but with great relish
in delighted, globby handfuls.

We'd have infinite patience
repeating the same simple phrases
over and over again
and mopping up the spills.

If our relationship was a baby
it would already be bonded
with both of us.
At this age, it would scream and cry
when we left it alone
or didn't feed it enough
or even if we forgot to give it attention.
Sometimes it would get cranky.
Sometimes it would have a load in its diaper.
Sometimes it would keep us from sleeping
all night long.
We'd know this stage wouldn't last forever
and love it anyhow.

If our relationship was a baby
it would already have a few useful skills
it would be very good at:
making us smile and laugh and sing
helping us to play
making us talk baby talk and produce funny noises
keeping us thinking
seriously about the future.

If our relationship was a baby
there'd be no question about its
absolute and definite and
permanent
belonging in the world.

We'd show it off to everyone.
We'd know it was here to stay.
It would still need changing
three or four times a day
and have plenty of growing to do
but we'd have no doubt
that it would become
wiser and brighter
more capable and more delightful
with every passing year.
We'd assume it would still be around
ten or twenty years from now
having a life of its own
turning out fine.

Margaret Cardea Black

PERSONALS

I want a woman lithe and long of limb,
I want a woman silent hour by hour,
So taken is she by a voice within.
I want a woman thinking not of me, but
Of a thousand things her own; I want
A woman steady at the bone. I want
Her love and mine a single thread;
I want us blithe in bed—and out—

Full confident. I want to lie
And look at her, and she at me,
Astonished at our luck, but wordlessly
Agreed to keep our talk material,
Mundane—the stuff of poems.

                                        Dogs
Bark, cats lick our feet, rain sluices
From the roof, the gutters leak, we
Light a fire. Ablaze, I kiss her cheek.

I want a woman lithe and long of limb,
Who laughs before she kisses back—
Or not—according to her whim.
I want a woman taken from within.

Burying the Cat

You write to say you love me, to say
I loved you; to tell me that even now
If I called your name you would come back;
To say you are empty, to say you want me,
That I want you—which is all true.

But, tonight, I am a grave digger,
Filling a small black hole with leaves,
With leaf-mold, with my cat, who is cold.

If I answered your letter I would say
To you that limitless love sets limits;
That though I miss your mouth on mine,
This emptiness in which I find myself is
Filling and good, that I am satisfied
In the way that a cat is satisfied
With its own solitude. I would tell you
That this grave I here fill is not the
Ultimate black hole, but is a cradle,
Cat-size, a bed; that the stone I lay
At its head says I am not forgetful,
That love lives on. I would remind you
Of what you already know, that grief
Is real and must be suffered, that wish
And deed are not the same. I would say
I want you—and will not call your name.

Nancy Boutilier

Because They Are Mine

I am not a man
trapped in a woman's body,
but a woman held prisoner
in a world
expecting me to fit
into uncomfortable shoes
and walk with a certain swing of the hips
along roads that lead to alien pastures.

Call it perspiration or sweat,
but know that it is wet, just the same.
My glow is laced
with grit and grease
from the front axle.
It's my car,
so I fix it,
and then I fix
dinner
and wash the laundry,
happy to hang her sweaters and socks to dry.
When I have time,
I alternate her underwear on the line
with mine,
knowing that nobody cares but me.
I have only myself to please,
and I enjoy tinkering, creating, rebuilding.
I love the songs that spin from my bicycle
after I've freshly packed the bearings,
the melody my cat purrs when I stroke
the thick fur surrounding his ears.
I love the smell that kicks
when my chain saw chews pine
as much as a fresh cut of roses.
I rock with pleasure
at the silent rhythms my body finds
shoveling snow, walking in sand,
and breathing beside the woman I love.
I revel in the salty taste of sweat
hanging on my upper lip

when my work demands it.
All responses are womanly
because they are mine.
I have only myself to please,
and it pleases me to love her.

Olga Broumas

Sometimes, as a Child

when the Greek sea
was exceptionally calm
the sun not so much a pinnacle
as a perspiration of light, your brow and the sky
meeting on the horizon, sometimes

you'd dive
from the float, the pier, the stone
promontory, through water so startled
it held the shape of your plunge, and there

in the arrested heat of the afternoon
without thought, effortless
as a mantra turning
you'd turn
in the paused wake of your dive, enter
the suck of the parted waters, you'd emerge

clean caesarean, flinging
live rivulets from your hair, your own
breath arrested. Something immaculate, a chance

crucial junction: time, light, water
had occurred, you could feel your bones
glisten
translucent as spinal fins.

In rain-
green Oregon now, approaching thirty, sometimes
the same
rare concert of light and spine
resonates in my bones, as glistening
starfish, lover, your fingers
beach up.

She Loves

deep prolonged entry with the strong pink cock,
the situps it evokes from her, arms fast
on the climbing invisible rope to the sky,
clasping and unclasping the cosmic lorus.

Inside, the long breaths of lung and cunt
swell the vocal cords and a rasp a song,
loud sudden overdrive into disintegrate,
spinal melt, video hologram in the belly.

Her tits are luminous and sway to the rhythm
and I grab them and exaggerate their orbs.
Shoulders above like loaves of heaven,
nutmeg-flecked, exuding light like violet diodes

closing circuit where the wall, its fuse box,
so stolidly stood. No room for fantasy.
We watch ourselves transform the past
with such disinterested fascination,

the only attitude that does not stall
the song by an outburst of consciousness
and still lets consciousness, loved and incurable
voyeur, peek in. I tap. I slap. I knee, thump, bellyroll.

Her song is hoarse and is taking me,
incoherent familiar path to that self we are all
cortical cells of. Every o in her body
beelines for her throat, locked on

a rising ski-lift up the mountain, no
grass, no mountaintop, no snow.
White belly folding, muscular as milk.
Pas de deux, pas de chat, spotlight

on the key of G, clef du roman, tour de force letting,
like the sunlight lets a sleeve worn against wind, go.

Skylight

Lie here, you say.
The clouds are sailing by.
The wind's picked up.

Careful not to touch, I stretch
along your body, place my head
a fraction of an inch from yours

inside the small square
of light-charged air
that heats your comforter.

Look up, you murmur,
See the way they slide?
I watch, grow dizzy with the pace

as white silks slip across
the turquoise frame, as your cool breath
moves moist against my ear.

This is where I love
to lie and dream, you say. And here's
the moment I could tell you

I've been dreaming too, of you,
or simply turn my face
and meet your lips,

the moment I could trust
I understand your hints,
and why you've brought me
to this place.

And if I kissed you
softly as a cloud,
traveled over you
as slowly as a mist,

and entered you
as gentle as a fog,
would I be
as welcome as a rain?

Would you lie still,
watch sky as if I
wasn't touching you?
Would you run?

Or would you sigh,
so glad to have
the waiting done,
and turn to me,

and could we two,
together, gather
like a storm?

As You Fly to Chicago: A Confession

—for Janice

Before you left, I bought another chain
so your quartz ornament could pendant down
between your breasts, and weight the hollow place
I like to lay my hand to calm your breath.

I know I often give you what I need.
And now you're gone, and I'm a wishbone sprung,
an unhinged sternum with its ribs all slipped
and disengaged, the flopping heart uncaged.

I wander like I'm lost around our house,
from desk to yard to empty bed and back
—which means the joke's on me when I admit
that I could hardly wait for you to leave.

I saw a part of me who would emerge
in solitude: the hard-edged writer gone
too flaccid from the comforts of your love,
who longed to keen and howl about the house

and rattle back to skeletal remains
of pain's incisive easy eloquence,
instead of groping to articulate
the brinkless sloppy liquid of our love.

Janice, remember diagrams we drew
in grade school, shading in to show how deep
two circles intersect? I'm scared to find
how far you've cast yourself across my life.

If our relationship is like two spheres
that deeply overlap, am I eclipsed,
the part that's "us" what love has penciled in,
so when you leave I'm like a bitten moon?

We both run cringing at the sound of "wife,"
its specter draped with aprons, dresses, men.
But I need words to show I mean to stay,
to say how very deep in me you spin.

Fly back to me, and lay your palm against
this heart that spills itself in search of you.
Your hand completes the line that marks my edge
and lets me recognize my life's own breath.

Two Songs for Touch

I. Sleeping with You

Tenderest: your soft stroked
        cheek beside my breast,
my kiss there. Then you stretch
        and let me tumble,
                nestled, toward your chest.

Your palm supports my neck
        and I remember
how to float again, to let
        the body rest and trust
                this water, willingness.

You tug on me as surely
        as a newborn's suck
knots up the womb again,
        beloved draw that rakes
                and heals old emptiness.

II. Skin

Hands to cup a chin and cheek,
Lips to trace a nape of neck,

Hips to fit a belly's curve,
Words to witness what we have.

I used to say *A pillow pressed*
against my chest will pass for touch.

But now to press along your spine,
reach over you and cup your breast—

I'll never know a better rest.

Melissa Cannon

Rondel du Jour

She takes her coffee hot and dark and sweet;
her lovers, spicy (pink lips rimmed in salt).
She licks the sauce from veins of bright cobalt
around the finest porcelain. Her meat—

the oyster, which she tends to overeat,
but who would call such gluttony a fault?
She takes her coffee hot and dark. And sweet-
skinned lovers, spicy, pink lips rimmed in salt,

spread like warm honey across her cool smooth sheet,
consume delicious hours and exalt
the tongue and palate with love's heady malt;
then, for another early morning treat,
she takes her coffee—hot and dark and sweet.

Lori Cardona

Note to My Lover's Brother

There is a tense, exquisite moment
after our good-night kiss
and before the "I love you"
when I wait

Suspended
my breath held in
I find myself in so much love
and loving that good-night kiss

Maybe there will be another
and another after that
maybe we'll begin to touch
I wait to follow her lead

I used to push impatiently
I used to question why
I tried to understand her pain
as she switched from hot to warm

My sweet and tender lover
she can only let go
when she's free to let go
and I love her even more

So now the wait is fine with me
I've learned to be trustworthy
I've learned to truly feel and see
I've learned to understand

The reward is great
as my heart expands
it's better than my dreams
because I can hold back

although you did not
I will not push her
you've done that enough
I will not use her

You've already used
she is my life, my love, my heart
I will still be here
when all she sees is me

And you are a nightmare forgotten

Anything

it's the least I can do
about the way I feel

I always notice
her dirty white car
needs washing badly
but she shouldn't have to
do anything like that

nothing dirty for her
no scrubbing tubs or toilets floors or dishes
no laundry sweeping or painting of walls
no cat box cleaning
no tired feet no aching back
nothing too hard or unpleasant

I'd get out there under the sun
in my T-shirt and shorts
with a bucket some sponges a hose
spray her car down with water
soap it up good scrub off all the dirt
so the hood shines bright
then dry it off quick with soft towels
rub the streaks from the windows
till I see my sweaty face blinking back at me
polish the rims paint black on the tires

I'd go at the interior with a vacuum
shake out the floor mats empty the ashtray
but of course she's too smart to smoke
wipe down every surface take Q-Tips to each
groove and vent remove all the crud and dust

I'd try to make her car
look as good and clean as she does
for a car that is
so she'll be smiling
and pleased to ride inside there

that's about as much
as you can do for a woman
who's already got a lover
and a dirty car

TO HOLD ME INSIDE OUT

Look at her hands,
the calm expression on her face—
do you see how she understands

me? I had to have
the chance to be her mate,
to look at her hands

continuously. They craft a precious
plan to consume me in her fate.
Don't you know she understands

there isn't any man
who could compete in this race?
Just look at her hands

and listen to her laugh.
In my life she moves with grace.
Do you see she understands

what fits inside my hand
is finer than being straight?
Look at her soft hands
on my skin. An emotional embrace
is what we understand.

Laura Castellanos del Valle

Last Kiss

To avoid the thought
of never kissing you again,
I try to remember the goodbye
I didn't recognize as farewell.
A rapid see-you-later glance
of lips. Motor idling.
I insist on another last
kiss, more tender. One unfamiliar
with hurry or acquainted with rush.

Your kisses caved my knees
and scaled my desires.
In elevators I prayed
for mechanical failures. In public
I wished us invisible.
Pinned to the nearest wall
by your tongue I was mounted
butterfly preserved in flight.
Prized in your collection.

But these are all
set the scene, twist the plot,
kisses. Can I recollect
the final spectacle? Saturday
morning salad tossed with linens,
cups, newspapers, and Friday
clothes. Which kiss prelude
to the sweet exhaustion of love
was epilogue to my dreams?

Missing You

I am slightly deranged
from missing you. Minor
misalignments of motion and meaning
unhinge me.

I have collected your hairs
from the brush on the dresser
in an effort to weave a tiny you.

I have named one of the pillows for you.
Confused by the relentless
passage of day to night, I forget
the particulars and call them all dear.

Without you here I have grown
a beard underneath each arm
and sideburns on my legs.

I have traded in the Technicolor
for chiaroscuro. Lost the last chapter
of the Gothic. Checked in
as a winter guest at a summer hotel.

I tap out your number
and sneak through your empty
rooms in sound waves.

Not finding your scent in the living
room, I return to the closet
for your salmon chamois shirt.
I wear it and take us out for dinner.

YOU ASK ME FOR A LOVE NAME

for Pat

I name you moon bird   diamond frost   night fruit
tender flag   bramble nest   vision bread   proud eye
I call you flying your tongue lifts me radiant
fills lost places
I swallow you staining my mouth sweet
with your blackberry nipples
I raise you over my house proclaim you
Clasp your head burrowing between my legs
I paint you watch you like mountains at dusk
Let you
whenever you want with a rush of blue violet spring
I name you darkness which heals
moving over my weariness in stars
I guard you
face you
polish you
Name you pirate with kidnapping grin
I name you fire & fine
I name you this glistening brilliant plumage
I put on my wings
crowing

Your Fingers Are Still

inside me pulsing
as I vacuum   look at books   wash dishes   cook
ride down the road   open my mail   burn the trash
Your fingers buckle
my knees   Stomach turns over   small moans
escape my lips at the laundromat   grocery store
Your tongue shivering me while I call a new job
pull the covers up on my bed   go to the bank
Smack of your comforting belly as you come on me
as I catch a ferry   iron a shirt   pull weeds
Your fingers don't stop
moving me

This Is

the blackberry jam I picked & boiled in swift sky August
mooning over your arrival in November
I imagined with sweet anticipation licking
the corners of your mouth dark with fruit
smiling as your soft Brooklyn voice
murmurs *You made this? Really?*
Yes I wandered searching for the fattest ones
their skins gleaming purple
tearing my bare arms as I reached   stooped
my fingers crimson & rose madder
planning to stir you

as I watched the limpid water wash silver to shore
Sun a blur in these blue swallow arrows of desire
I made this jam sure of your pleasure
thinking of your fingers & lips stained with me
I left it tart pungent as this longing
to spread you sweetly over me

Elizabeth Clare

HOW TO TALK TO A NEW LOVER ABOUT CEREBRAL PALSY

Tell her: *Complete strangers*
have patted my head, kissed
my cheek, called me courageous.

Tell this story more than once, ask
her to hold you, rock you
against her body, breast to back,

her arms curving round, only
you flinch unchosen, right arm trembles.
Don't use the word *spastic.*

In Europe after centuries
of death by exposure
and drowning,
they banished us
to the streets.

Let her feel the tension burn down your arms,
tremors jump. Take it slow: when she asks
about the difference between CP and MS,

refrain from handing her an encyclopedia.
If you leave, know that you will ache.
Resist the urge to ignore your body. Tell her:

They taunted me retard, cripple,
defect. *The words sank into my body.*
The rocks and fists left bruises.

> Gimps and crips, caps
> in hand, we still
> wander the streets but now
> the options abound: telethons,
> nursing homes, and welfare lines.

Try not to be ashamed as you flinch and tremble
under her warm hands. Think of the stories
you haven't told yet. Tension grips fierce.

Ask her what she thinks as your hands shake
along her body, sleep curled against her,
and remember to listen: she might surprise you.

Tremors

My hands, their knobby knuckles, I tuck them
against my body, let tremors run
from shoulder blade to fingertip. Tension
burns the same track of muscles, pencil slows
across blue-lined paper: my words dance
like sandpiper tracks at low tide.
Kids call cripple. Bank tellers stare silent.
Doctors predict arthritis. Joints crack
to the grip of tremor and tension:
my hands want to learn to swear. Late at night
as I trace the long curve of your body,
tremors touch skin, reach inside,
and I expect to be taunted, only to have you
rise beneath my hands and ask for more.

Cheryl Clarke

Buttons

I wanted to unbutton every piece of your clothing
which was all buttons
from that silk shirt
down to the crotch of that gaberdine skirt.
My buttons too:
my jeans brass-button up,
my shirt has six shell buttons,

my camisole has three tiny ones.
This restaurant is in my way
when I want to be unbuttoned
and unbuttoning.
Can't you tell?
To do it now.
To reach across the bread.
To start unbuttoning.
My arms so long.
My fingers faster than the eye and omnidextrous.
Now, ain't that loving you?

NOTHING

Nothing I wouldn't do for the woman I sleep with
when nobody satisfy me the way she do.

kiss her in public places
win the lottery
take her in the ass
in a train lavatory
sleep three in a single bed
have a baby
to keep her wanting me.

wear leather underwear
remember my dreams
make plans and schemes
go down on her in front of her
other lover

give my jewelry away
to keep her wanting me.

sell my car
tie her to the bed post and
spank her
lie to my mother
let her watch me fuck my other lover
miss my only sister's wedding
to keep her wanting me.

buy her cocaine
show her the pleasure in danger
bargain
let her dress me in colorful costumes
of low cleavage and slit to the crotch
giving easy access
to keep her wanting me.

Nothing I wouldn't do for the woman I sleep with
when nobody satisfy me the way she do.

Martha Courtot

TWO THIEVES

my phantom lover
you sneak into my house
in the middle of the afternoon
between my daughter's piano lesson
and your own motherly duties
and here you are sitting on my bed grinning

are you real
or have I imagined you from longing so well?

phantom lover,
your body is real enough in my hands
the trees outside my window blush
the neighbors cringe
even after you leave, my hands follow you
you will feel them while you stand at the stove cooking
while you sit at the table talking
while you read in your bed at night
a dark red blush will rise from your center

oh my blue-eyed phantom lover
in this hour when you are with me,
your fierce, powerful body over mine,
the Saint of Thieves watches over us
she helps us to steal this pleasure
from under our children's noses
how easily she convinces us
we will never have to pay

now we have made the afternoon wicked
with our cries
we have changed the complexion of the day
everything alive rises around us throbbing
like our lips after an hour of kissing
the walls pulse and throb pulse and throb
your body over mine changes the color
of my eyes forever
you crave a piece of me

to carry away with you
my breast is willing to go
it is so in love with your mouth

when you have gone
night comes quickly
my body is lonely
meanwhile the thief in me
folds the great thing I have stolen
from respectable day
into my dark center

inside me a great smile rises up

Patricia Donegan

SPECIAL DELIVERY

I've gone through the bardos of bloated
   Indian bodies floating on the Ganges

gone through smoky midnight blues bars of Chicago

paged through 100,000 books of monks' ink

slept in Korean marketplaces next to drying fish
   in summer & huddled under quilts in winter

looked up at the moon through rain & haze

licked thousands of bread crumbs & no bread crumbs
   from my callused fingers

exhausted millions of cells through lifetimes of
passion, aggression & ignorance

contorted my body into different positions: crossed,
bent, stretched, rolled, jerked, turned, shit,
made love, had babies, moved fast as a deer
crossing a road & sat still as a steller's jay

looked into the eyes of the "enemy" in China,
Ireland & Mexico before the moment of death

held the hands of newborns, marveled at their tiny
fingernails, held the hands of ones just dead

I've gone through this & more

to deliver this rose petal to you.

So This Is Love

Snow
all afternoon
deep, silent

the creek water
barely audible
outside the window

I slammed
the refrigerator door
with everything I've got:

"I don't want you sleeping
with anybody else,"
I screamed,

you hugged me
& picked up the broken mayonnaise jar
from the floor.

Lover's Wish

When I'm dead
steal my bones
cut them up
into Chinese carvings
a mountain, a sage
a heart, a leaf
to hang like stars
in the sky.

When I'm dead
make from my bones
a whistle for a child
a necklace to fondle at night
the dagger geishas use
behind silken screens
an incense burner
a comb for your hair
tangled on the pillow
a netsuke, smooth, soft
as mother's breast,

most of all make
a small clown face
that laughs a millennium.

When I'm dead
make art of my bones
bleach & dry them in the sun
pure white
startling as stars
turned round in your hand
like a porcelain cup,
then after holding my bones

my skull, arms, pelvis & feet
take my thigh bone
gently
make a flower vase.

Amy Edgington

THE BUTCH SPEAKS

Set aside the clothes,
the swagger, the roles
and it comes down to this:
in my dreams, I am most often
butch, which is to say, that you,
beloved, are the fish on a hook,
pulling the whole damn boat.

Awake, when I kiss you with my eyes
across the restaurant table,
I know what I most anticipate,
and, no, I don't mean the lasagne.
I mean the fuse that joins our lips,
nipples, tongues and groins.
In my mind I'm playing
with matches.

Dream Lover

Skin to skin in the bow of your bed,
we drift a river of bliss in no
particular hurry to reach the sea.
This time I cradle your back;
my breath feathers the nape of your neck.
Your breasts are fuller than I'd remembered.
I slide my hand over the unexpected mound of your belly.

I never touched you when you were pregnant.
I was the one you loved before
you married and had three babies.
Now I never see you except in dreams
as regular and vivid as my blood.

You will always be the first woman I loved
without lies, and I'm still in love with the me
who loved you like an animal and a god.
Since then I've been threatened and abused,
I've been loved more kindly and more wisely.

In my waking life I rarely kiss
without thought of consequence.

But in my dreams I lean toward you
in front of lighted windows
with night coming on.
In my dreams we still stroll
hand in hand across the campus,
exciting envy as much as hate,
and our courage never flags.

Once I dreamt we were old, both widows.
Meeting again after thirty years,
I tell you I've been faithful
through a lifetime apart.

Ana Bantigue Fajardo

Island Dream

Long ago before the whites came
you watched me
from afar
as I paddled my *banca*
up on to the shore
returning from a fishing trip.
You noticed the way
my muscles
tightened

as I drove my paddle
gently through
the ocean waters.
My brown skin
perfectly baked from
the tropical sun,
my rich black hair
dripping with seawater
and sweat—
You noticed the
intensity of my Pinay—
Pilipina eyes—
the way I was one with
my canoe
            with my paddle
            with our mother sea
You waited for me
to ride the wave in,
and you watched as
I slipped my *sarong* off
and lay on the sand
to rest.
You noticed the way
my breasts were
flawlessly molded—
Parang Mayon Volcano,
ang inisip mo. Kay ganda.
How beautiful—you thought.
It was then you could wait no longer
so you approached me.

Malacas na babae, kailangan ko kita.
Strong woman, I need you.

Lori Faulkner

First of the Motorcycle Poems

you
soft in your leather
not quite a
bike dyke
no studs on your jacket
but
oh
those gloves are sinful
long
black
leather
with
zippers
no less
so butch
of you
to have those gloves

so femme

of you

to have those eyes

Second of the Motorcycle Poems

At night, in my dreams,
my legs and thighs
spin a cocoon
around her
and there is a penis
slender and firm
it slides gently into me
and I hold her there

In daylight
she appears in front of me
leaning against
her classic black
BMW motorcycle
leather jacket
denim jeans
on her boy body
raking five
juvenile delinquent fingers
through her short dark hair
she is my teenage guy
in different times
I could be gun moll
to her gangster moves

a cigarette dangles
from her seductive
heart-stopping lips

When I hold her wrists
above her head
and take her with my tongue
the smell of her strong and wild
as the best acid trip
When I feel the outside curve
of her breasts
soft as my heart melting
at the sight of
her citrine almond eyes
we know the truth together
it's an inside joke
When they call her butch
and rate her high on the scale
I call her my woman
and take what I want.

We Always Were

Missing you
remembering hips that used to call to me
lips that stopped my heart
swelled my womanness to overflowing
Missing you

remembering nights and mornings
when we lay together
planning things we'd do that day
but neither of us moving
except
into
each other's
everything

souls communing
walking
through
our inner gardens
tasting blossoms   fruit
blooming in our tropics
touching forests   evergreen
rising from our heat
raining berries petals magic leaves
finding pollen

left on luscious lips
of sistahs loving sistahs

SONNET

I loved you as if we had touched
the billowing air that spun our fresh-mown
thoughts: heady August, your amber eyes like rays.
Leonine, you watched me: deeply shaded and alone.
I loved the sparks of grass, pale green and blonde,
flung wide as you rolled down the length of lawn.
We walked the steep, damp path to the pond,
divided the surface into lines on the face
of difference, the softening creases
round your joints, my large hope like the water between us.
Gray head tipped water-dark, I watched
you go and swam hard into acceptance
wanting exhaustion and a map for distance.
I loved you as if we had touched.

MAIN LINE

para Alba

Caffè latte
with a
sprinkle
of
chocolate
baits me
with
your
honey morphine
smile
of
ambivalence.

First
hot,
then
cold.

I
want
you
to
burn
for me.

Stretching
my
desire
until it
rips
whole.

Proud
to be
easy.

I
realize
possession
is a
drug related
crime.

I would do the time.

Lynn Goldfarb

Poem With an Attitude

You think I'm such
a nice girl

because I still write
sonnets sestinas even luv
poems

because I still don
camisoles pantyhose even sport
a bra

because I still shave
wear skirts mascara even carry
a purse

You think I'm so
straight polite frigid

Newsflash Babe

You've never seen me
in my half-zipped black jeans writing dyke poems
topless in the moonlight

You've never been inside my wilderness

You don't know
how my lips would sear your tattoo
turn it purple then red

You don't know
how hard   my hips   would throw
your ass   against the wall

You can't imagine
the frenzied circling   of my pelvis   my hands
my thighs'   merciless grip

I am not
a   nice   girl

And you
under all that   black   and metal
are as soft   as a chocolate

k i s s

in the noonday sun

Jewelle Gomez

My Chakabuku Mama

My first big love was cosmically correct:
she rolled perfect joints, made herbal tea
and vegetarian chili.
We sat on huge pillows talking hours on end
about the cosmic connection, the state of the union
and who should do the laundry
in an equal relationship.

We meditated on celestial seasonings
and I pretended to comprehend
numerology, graphology, phrenology
and the phases of the moon.
I slept with my head facing north
abiding a vicious draft.
My shoes sat outside the door
crying to be let in.
We searched together for the higher ground
through macrobiotic bushes and abstinence;
me peering into her thick transcendental glasses
she facing Mecca.

We chanted to find our center
beneath an azure blue candle from Key Food
and sprinkled a pinch of salt
in the four corners of each room.
We never separated
without talking it all out
or allowed bad vibes to invade our space.
She made breakfast on alternate Sundays
and I never drank gin.
We went on camping trips every spring.
I read poets and journals
and loaned all of my favorite clothes
to slight acquaintances.
I never eavesdropped
when she talked on the phone.
I ate fresh fruit
and only argued with Con Edison.

I cut my finger nails.
We played kalimba duets.
I learned to love brown rice
and Japanese slippers.
I threw out my Salems.
She threw out the roach spray.
We shuddered in unison at the mention
of french fries or Table Talk pies.
I never watched TV
or listened to James Brown.
I gave up aspirin and wore 100% cotton,
had my tarot read, meditated on a tatami bed,
ate raw fish and burned patchouli.
She could squeeze the names of three
Egyptian goddesses
into any general conversation.
Malice and jealousy beat a hasty retreat
from my consciousness. Our life moved forth
on a path of righteous awareness and sisterhood.
Then she left me flat.
Exiting serenely
on a cloud of universal love.

Keystone

for Diane

The first picture you take of me
in our new home I am sitting in front
of the huge, unworking fireplace. Laughing
at nothing in particular: the boxes
are finally unpacked, there's no more dust.
That we are finally together.
I'm not posed or self-conscious of the gap
in my teeth. I'm usually afraid
it makes me look loud, unladylike.
I seem to be in motion, shaking
with hilarity.
Behind me the impressive masonry
of the hearth. Handcrafted bricks, reddish brown
snuggled tight with creamy beige, some smooth
others textured as if still in the quarry.
They build, each upon the one before. Worn
to match, colors distinct but grown together.
They have such straight, mortared angles
yet they curve to frame an arc,
now shuttered until work can be done.
They feel fluid.
Suspended at their center, the keystone, not
classically shaped but muted double triangles
wedged one atop the other. Their sharp points removed
to make the union easier.

Who I Am

Making love to you
I felt for the first time
I am a woman who loves women
and for the first time
felt I am right here
right now doing what I most
want to do
with who I most want to do it
I could do it with the lights on or off
I could take it hot under the covers
or cold on top
wide awake
in my right mind
totally lost   totally loved
loving who I am   who I'm with
separate   together
forever or just for now
it doesn't matter to me
just the great splashy feeling of you coming
and me knowing
this is who I am

Trouble

How 'bout if I just
lift your three winter sweaters
let my head rest between your breasts
lick your nipples up into tiny pyramids
just for a moment
nobody needs to know
your lover or mine
how 'bout
run my palms down the smooth length of your sides
armpit to ankles
like two long runways
my hands could fly
lifting for take-off before they even reach
the curve of your instep
hold each toe
put my finger in between every one
how 'bout   nobody needs to know
your lover or mine
feel the light hairs down
in the small of your back
run my tongue up your spine
I'm not afraid of bumps in the road
I could really go the distance
how 'bout   just for a moment
I nip the nape of your neck
walk my lips along the line of your jaw
make butterflies with our eyes
lashes fluttering together so close

we open wide and see
one eye
each
get to know the other's scent
your lover or mine gets to all the time
how 'bout
just for a moment
I bury my nose in your coconut hair
feel you
get wet

nobody
needs to know

Adele Gorelick

SWEET DREAMS

"World's Greatest Husband" we joked.
I bought a blue-ribbon badge
With that message
To give you at our last July 4th,
My divorce final.
My Independence Day.
Your badge for me read,
"Thank you."

Now I sleep alone.
In the arms of a corduroy pillow

Made for sitting up in bed,
And called by some a "husband."

We piled my red one
On your black one.
Obscene.
Naughty.
Ineffective.
As we tried to make you comfortable
Six months into cancer.

Nothing helped.
Not even a thousandfold
Soluble salts of opium.
Only the pain rocked you,
Though we tried arms, kisses,
Pressing your hand,
Your sons and I,
Pulling your oxygen mask
To ease you into sleep.

My Cynic

"You're keeping a journal,
Aren't you?" you asked,
As I sat reviewing a report for work.
"All the leftover cancer lovers
Write those books.
Then they go around speaking
And get rich."

You were wrong, my dearest love.
You are gone:
Your lips,
Your creamy thighs,
Your knowing hands.
I am rich with memories,
Photos, gifts, friends, and your sons,
But poor.
As lost as wasted pages
Strewn when words do nothing
To fill my empty life.

Visit Me

I love it when you come.
Don't stop.

At noon the wind blowing open the door.
I knew it was you.
To enjoy the snow.

To see we were okay.
As before,
When you came as a bird
Fluttering between the front windows
After we buried you under the trees
In Rock Creek Park.

I love it when you come.
Don't stop.

When you first died,
I heard you in sounds:
The cats at Marge and Anne's
Crying for food
As you screamed in pain.
The rush of the sea
Obeying the tide
Your screams, too.

But lately a fragile balance:
Son Jeff gleeful
At the first hockey score
After a long strike.
Your same wild unloosed joy.

I love it when you come.
Don't stop.

And friend Pat hearing fireworks
In Baltimore New Year's Day.
To keep me company.
To fill the void.
Shouting, "Yes!" like you.

I love it when you come.
Don't stop.

Janice Gould

MY CRUSH ON THE YAKIMA WOMAN

It was raining along the Columbia River
that November I lived on the farm.
One morning at 6:00 A.M. the Yakima woman
drove the gravel road to my place.
She had come to pick me up.

She was sure pretty, that woman,
with her wide face, obsidian eyes,
and hair the color of blackbird wings.
She had slim long legs, and every guy
at the cannery where we worked
was sick for her.
But it was me she took home
to meet her kids.

Her husband was out hunting that weekend.
I saw him only once
when he came home, changed clothes,
and went off with a beer in his hand.

She waved good-bye,
not bothering to get up.
I strummed my guitar.
She listened and smoked.
Then she said, "Sing some more."
So I threw back my head
and sang "Your Cheatin' Heart"
in a way Patsy Cline would have understood.
And the Yakima woman thought about it,
smiled, and said, "That was real good."

So I played and drank,
sang and cried. Finally
she asked, "Do you want to go to bed?"
She did not mean with her.

I slept on the sofa,
she slept in her thin chemise.
The kids slept scattered all over the floor.
About four in the morning I got up
and looked at the sky. It angered me
to see it cold and full of stars
above the black fir forest.

COMPANION

I chose a woman who would not disturb
the burning core of me.
She embraces fire so tenderly
my heart becomes a salmon and leaps
into her net of moist hair.

I chose a woman who would not deny
the heartswell of my singing.
She watches the ocean so lovingly
my heart becomes a red bird
in a winter tree.

I chose a woman who would not violate
the sacred trust of my body.
She regards me so steadily
my heart becomes a bell
clanging wildly in the wind.

I chose a woman who would not silence
the words of her own fierce longing.
She closes distances so exactly
my heart becomes a star
falling through the night sky.

I chose a woman who would not refuse
to mother my infancy.
Between her legs all things are born.
At her breast everything has life.
She cradles my head so soundly
my heart becomes an apple, burnished
and cool in her hand.

Kissing at the Counter

I was sitting in the office at my cold white desk.
The phone was hard—the pen solid. My work
heaped before me like unsorted laundry

        And I thought of you   The inside
of my skin felt warm   and the whole
world moved over to make room
for the memory   of your body and mine   mirroring
heat and heart beats

The office light stared down on me; bright and rude.
People popped out of their cubicles like jack-in-the-boxes—
wound up. Walking and talking

        And the whole world moved
over so that I could feel pillows
sinking   and tongues melting   and time
        tumbling

I picked up my handful of jangling keys and drove
my stubborn car across crowded parking lots
to where I slammed my blue door shut and shot
through the store where you stood
behind your counter, a pen behind
your ear, papers at your beck and call. You
were jotting things down and I looked at your unfinished
business in swarms on the crackling wood countertop and I
    forgot

everything except my dentist appointment
and my lunch hour ticking smaller and smaller
and the keys in my hand and the clock on the wall
and the socks in the hamper and the money in my wallet

        Until you said   Kiss me
And I leaned across the counter
and the whole world
moved aside

Valentine

for Chris

Starting with your hair. I love rumpling it up/Your strawberry blond hair that you call otherwise/The freckles you'd rather hide/Hiding out on Sunday with you in bed/You in bed/Bedtime on nights when we cuddle/Cuddled up with you, your heart beating against my back/Your heart/Your big generous heart that breaks easily into tears/Your leaky faucet eyes that cry/You cried when my daughter lost her doll, Twinkle/The twinkle in your smile/Your child smile/You're a big child/Your love for my child/Your wild side/Your tame side/The part of you that makes me like to stay/Staying at home with you/making a home with you/Making love with you/Loving you

A FUNERAL: PLAINSONG FROM A YOUNGER WOMAN TO AN OLDER WOMAN

i will be your mouth now, to do your singing
breath belongs to those who do the breathing.
warm life, as it passes through your fingers
flares up in the very hands you will be leaving

you have left, what is left
for the bond between women is a circle
we are together within it.

i am your best, i am your kind
kind of my kind, i am your wish
wish of my wish, i am your breast
breast of my breast, i am your mind
mind of my mind, i am your flesh
i am your kind, i am your wish
kind of my kind, i am your best

now you have left you can be
wherever the fire is when it blows itself out.
now you are a voice in any wind
    i am a single wind
now you are any source of a fire
    i am a single fire

wherever you go to, i will arrive
whatever i have been, you will come back to
wherever you leave off, i will inherit
whatever i resurrect, you shall have it

you have right, what is right
for the bond between women is returning
we are endlessly within it
and endlessly apart within it.
it is not finished
it will not be finished

i will be your heart now, to do your loving
love belongs to those who do the feeling.

life, as it stands so still along your fingers
beats in my hands, the hands i will, believing
that you have become she, who is not, any longer
somewhere in particular

we are together in your stillness
you have wished us a bonded life
love of my love, i am your breast
arm of my arm, i am your strength
breath of my breath, i am your foot
thigh of my thigh, back of my back
eye of my eye, beat of my beat
kind of my kind, i am your best

when you were dead i said you had gone to the mountain

the trees do not yet speak of you

a mountain when it is no longer
a mountain, goes to the sea
when the sea dies it goes to the rain
when the rain dies it goes to the grain
when the grain dies it goes to the flesh
when the flesh dies it goes to the mountain

now you have left, you can wander
will you tell whoever could listen
tell all the voices who speak to younger women
tell all the voices who speak to us when we need it
that the love between women is a circle
and is not finished

wherever i go to, you will arrive
whatever you have been, i will come back to
wherever i leave off, you will inherit
whatever we resurrect, we shall have it
we shall have it, we have right

and you have left, what is left

i will take your part now, to do your daring
lots belong to those who do the sharing.
i will be your fight now, to do your winning
as the bond between women is beginning
in the middle at the end
my first beloved, present friend
if i could die like the next rain
i'd call you by your mountain name
and rain on you
want of my want, i am your lust

wave of my wave, i am your crest
earth of my earth, i am your crust
may of my may, i am your must
kind of my kind, i am your best

tallest mountain least mouse
least mountain tallest mouse

you have put your very breath upon mine
i shall wrap my entire fist around you
i can touch any woman's lip to remember

we are together in my motion
you have wished us a bonded life

a funeral: for my first lover and longtime friend
Yvonne Mary Robinson b. Oct. 20, 1939; d. Nov. 1974
for ritual use

DIFFERENCES

i

When the white woman
fell in love
with a Black woman

some of her friends said
isn't your life
hard enough?

as if to say

whatever happens
is your own
damned fault

ii

The first thing she noticed
was how people
stared

The second thing she noticed
was the way her friends
hesitated
when she introduced them
to her new lover

The third thing she noticed
was how often
they were seated in the backs
of restaurants
and how often
they received
bad service

The fourth thing she noticed
was an increasing sense
of isolation

The fifth thing she noticed
and the sixth
and the seventh
and the eighth

was every racist thing
anyone anywhere said

and the ninth
and the tenth
and the eleventh . . .

iii

Her family tried to put the world
into neat little boxes for her:
this is the good neighborhood
this is the bad neighborhood

She drives out of the *good*
neighborhood into the *bad*
neighborhood to visit
her lover

She hears the click
of her parents' voices
lock your door
lock your door
and the click
of car door locks
locking shut

She drives into
her lover's neighborhood
with the car doors unlocked
and the windows
open

iv

She remembers racist thoughts
she's had, she remembers
racist words she's said
she remembers racist things
she's done

The memories are toxins
seeping through her pores
She wants to cleanse herself,
flush them out

I am not a racist
I am not a racist

She is afraid
that one night
she will say something racist
in her sleep

v

The white woman's parents told her
she was lucky
she didn't look
Jewish
and she had
a *shikse* nose

The Black woman's parents told her
she was lucky
she was light-skinned
and she had
good hair

vi

Her lover tells her
you're not white
you're Jewish

This is a distinction
the white woman does
and does not
understand

The next time they fight
her lover calls her
white girl

vii

The white woman says

it's not just a matter
of different words
or different meanings

it's that sometimes
we're speaking
two different languages

and we don't even know it

viii

A group of men in a car rushing by them
screams out the window: *LEZZIES*
seeing only two women and a gesture
of tenderness, enough
to ascertain at 40 miles per hour
what name to call them, an unpleasant
but necessary reminder
of the one war
they fight together

ix

Sometimes when they were
dancing and watching each other's
eyes, it seemed that they had known
each other for years

Sometimes when they were
feasting on one of the meals
they cooked together,
it seemed that they had found
in each other a lost best friend,
a lost sister

Sometimes when they were
locked together, embracing,
it didn't seem possible
that they had been raised
to hate each other

Sometimes when they were
making love and only moonlight
lit the room, their skin
seemed to have the same color,
or rather, the same absence
of color

x

They sit next to each other
on the couch, watching a TV
documentary: white people
killing Black people.

A Black woman weeps, crouching
over the body of a young Black boy
lying in a river of blood.

White people
killing Black people.

The white woman feels the couch
split open
between them.

She wants to touch her lover's hand.
She doesn't.

xi

The Black woman says her hostility
is part of her heritage

she says it's not something
the white woman
can understand

no more white lovers
you're the last one

xii

The Black woman and the white woman
are walking down the street
holding hands.

The Black woman's arm
and the white woman's arm
form a V between them, the wings
of a bird taking flight, wings
like blades cutting the sky
into shreds, shreds like paper
falling on the heads
of all those who witness
this act.

The Black woman and the white woman
are walking down the street
holding hands.

xiii

In the kitchen, the Black woman
slices a challah.
The white woman is cooking
greens, the sweet smell of ham
rising from the pot.

She dreams the exchange
will always be this simple

She dreams
that their differences
will always be a source
of sustenance,
that they will always
feed each other

She dreams
of a long and beautiful
undisrupted feast.

A HOLLYWOOD ENDING

i will always connect you with that wretched
movie we saw on our last night together
another failed hollywood attempt to show real live
authentic lesbians   a lesbian's lover leaves her
in their first scene in the movie   that was all
we saw of their relationship   her grief
was ludicrous   and then of course there was
the inevitable gay bar scene looking like no gay bar
any of us has ever seen   two alleged dykes holding
pool cues   trying to look tough   one dressed
like paul revere   if i had known it would be
our last night together i would have made a different
choice   i never would have said, look i know this
movie's gonna be trash but we should see what
they're saying about us   we should see what's out there
if i had known   i would have picked something different
something respectable   a film i'd *want* to replay
in my mind   *desert hearts*   i'd connect you
with the thread of saliva between patricia charbonneau
and helen shaver's lips   or even *casablanca*
ingrid bergman's watery eyes in the final scene
cut to: the propeller   and back to: her watery eyes
if i had known that over and over i would replay

our last night together   if i had known that the last
time you'd ever hold my hand would be in the theater
where we saw that stupid movie   where we sank low
in our seats and you pulled my leg over yours and we
kept up a running commentary from beginning to end
like a lesbian siskel & ebert   two thumbs down
if i had known that the lesbian's grief over her
lost lover would mock me   parody my own grief
just the next day   if i had known i would have said
let's get the hell out of this insulting movie
full of lies   where lesbians don't look like lesbians
and don't even touch each other and go off and fuck men
if i had known   i would have said let's not waste
our last night together smirking and shaking our heads
at hollywood's distortions   if i had known that
real live authentic lesbian heartbreak was a mere
twelve hours away   if i had known   i would have
held your hand and not let go   i would have said
let's walk down that dark country road again   let's
kiss under the full moon one last time   let me
memorize the curve of your neck   i'll need it
to sustain me through the loneliness to come   if i had
known that soon i'd be missing you   if i had known

First, I want to make you come in my hand
while I watch you and kiss you, and if you cry,
I'll drink your tears while, with my whole hand, I
hold your drenched loveliness contracting. And
after a breath, I want to make you full
again, and wet. I want to make you come
in my mouth like a storm. No tears now. The sum
of your parts is my whole most beautiful
chart of the constellations—your left breast
in my mouth again. You know you'll have to be
your age. As I lie beside you, cover me
like a gold cloud, hands everywhere, at last
inside me where I trust you, then your tongue
where I need you. I want you to make me come.

You, little one, are just the kind of boy
I would have eyeballed at the bar, and cruised
efficiently, and taken home, and—used?
Hell, no! The bodice-busters say "enjoy,"
and how I do enjoy what girl you bring
back out in me, brought out in time for you
to riff all keys of titillation through
with those square, reddish hands whose quivering
sometimes on mine plucks songs from everything.

Bad, brash, and skinless, not a boy at all,
between boot-tops and that surprising small
waist is where my hands and mouth would slide,
effortless and attentive to you, guide
you, ride you to the place we both belong.

Julie Hall

FINDING THE DEER

In my room the murmur of the aquarium
echoed the circuitous path of my blood
recycling itself into muscles, fascia, tendons.
My heart drummed to the rhythm of the newts,
their bowed red-toed legs rotating,
grasping and pushing endlessly through the water,
searching out the rectangular space
in weightless orbit.
There with me in the tank's muted light
you were my lover, sexless:
I hadn't yet conceived of what you could be
until I found you one year,
like the deer I tracked as a kid
down a river in northern Michigan.
Wading barefoot I followed the icy creek for miles
through the July-dense forest,
pausing to run my finger
over the smooth shell of a basking turtle,

to dodge metallic-blue dragonflies
joined in frenzied copulation,
to admire tenuous winding flowers,
to pee. Until, in a moment,
the doe appeared with a crash:
Standing upright in the middle of the creek,
we stared at each other trembling, revealed.
That was the closest I had ever come to finding you
until I found myself
tracing the drama of your long-arch stomach,
when I discovered your sex, and mine;
when I understood for the first time how it could be
that you weren't a boy or a man,
and I wasn't a deer or a child.

First Love

Coat blown open,
eyes fixed on early April thunderheads,
you exhumed your secret
in a quiet steady steam
as if willing the words
to dissipate before I heard them.

Your uncle led you to the boathouse
though it was too cold to swim—

It took you all spring to tell me,
to discover the difference between me and him:
arms for arms, legs for legs,
setting in motion
everything coiled dormant
during childhood's solitary confinement.

—holding your hand as always,
but this day not looking at your face.

I remembered my baby-sitter when I was four:
the faint urine smell,
the smooth taut skin of his erection,
my tongue tracing
the corrugated tissue just beneath.

Inside he instructed you to lie down,
pull up your dress—

Your grandmother found you that day
and cleaned you up without a question,
telling your parents you had fallen on the swing.
Silence drifted in like snow
and they never heard a word you weren't saying.

—and, cheek resting on cool dirty cement,
he gutted you like a fish.

I was out of college when my grandmother told me,
nearly blind from her stroke:
she had seen my father "touch" me as a baby.
I never really believed it could be true.
Anyway, what's the difference
if it's me or you?

Jan Hardy

THE MOMENT BEFORE OUR LIPS CAME TOGETHER

it's a wish it's a hush a prayer
it's the best it's not possible
it keeps getting better you can break
all the rules of language and logic
just with your lips the softest the strongest
you can throw all the classics in the river
moby dick great expectations farewell to arms
you can write your own you can lift
my heart like an elevator up tall buildings faster
than a speeding cheetah my sweetheart
my hera you're lighter than air
you draw me like light you're the wealth
i always wanted and the knowledge
i was seeking my lifesaver my suntan
my house by the sea my celebration
and champagne in the midst of the everyday
you're an arrow of anger to pierce
through confusion your smile
cuts through crap like the sun
through clouds i want to
shine with you forever
drink you up dress you up
in the best dyke fashions
plastic money can buy
baby i want to baby you

mother you in a world free from Freud
Falwell, Helms and Rush
let's live in Michigan and wash
our plates in cold water
make love in a tent
and watch our breasts droop lower each year
and each time we kiss
i'll think of the first time
the moment before our lips came together
when all the world stretched out its arms
and we laughed, and jumped in

WILD HONEY

nights when
we don't expect it,
when we're tired and it's late
and tomorrow's work
waits to burst out of the alarm clock,
i turn off the light,
turn to you in bed
for a goodnight kiss and all
the air between us catches fire,
draws us into light and music,
colors playing over our skin,
and there is no first or second
now and then or give and take,
there's touch and taste and both of us
wanting, both of us filled,

water pouring from one cup into another
and back again, your sweet rain
opens my small wet flower, mine
opens yours, kisses like flowers
breathe the length of our bodies,
our legs and arms
grow wild roots around each other,
we drink the wine we stored for each other
ready, to our surprise, barely contained
while our heads were being sensible,
automatic and dull as drones,
our bodies were sensing the low hum,
the sweet scent, the rhythm,
soft petals sweating in the sun
all the while, we were
lifting up wings to the warm wind,
carousing, vibrating, diving,
dancing the wild honey dance all day.

Doris L. Harris

Quality Time

It's been
five months
an awful scare
a hysterectomy
a bought house

since you last reached for me,
so I be damned if I waste a moment
on foreplay
sweet dear woman, I need you
in the best way
so badly that my taste buds ache,
tonight,
when we climb into the bed
leave those pajamas on the floor
shut, lock and bolt the door
you can turn off the lights
or you can leave them on
the second it takes to do either,
is a second too long

Climb Inside of Me

I told my woman,
I said,
Woman I ain't in the mood
for no, girl to girl love
the kind that's only made
when the moon is full, and the cat is fed
I've been waiting for you
on the edge of the bed,
there is a stairwell to the left
a ladder to your right, take any route you like
but, you hurry and climb inside of me,
I need to feel your body weight

pressing into mine, as I tear at the flesh
on your round behind, Please
Now, don't go P. C. all over me
I want to hear you call out my name,
along with God's, Jesus, and all twelve apostles
let's not wrestle with semantics
there ain't no other way to say it
there ain't no other way to claim it,
except to say, I need some woman to woman love
some of that sweat pouring, politically incorrect
arching my back
taking no prisoners
neighbors banging on the wall, kind of love
need you ready and willing,
to come and climb
inside
of me.

Mary Diane Hausman

A BORN-AGAIN WIFE'S FIRST LESBIAN KISS

The first time I kissed my best friend,
fireworks went off.
Really. I heard them.
Years of pent up repression
plus weeks of mounting tension
let loose in one firecracker moment.

In my mind grew the image
of my head blowing off.

Our lips, forced together
by some magnetic pull,
one set of curved flesh toward the other,
the force of two struggling hearts
below those lips, little bird hearts
beating quickly, quickly,
wanting to explode.

The kiss was soft and knowing.
Our lips knew where to go.
The kiss was hard and had a punch.
The punch of forbidden fruit.
That, if-you-do-you'll-go-to-hell-
but-if-you-don't-you'll-die-
so-what's-the-difference
kind of punch.
Right in the mouth.

When we were able to pull our faces
away from each other,
to look at what we had done,
the fire was unbearable.
The fire in her blue eyes,
the fire on her cheeks;
the air, and our breath
fanned the flames on our faces
and caught fire again.

All I knew was I would
never be the same.
And she better
get the hell out of there
before my husband came home.

Six Years Ten Months

What would you like to do on the eighth day of April
When the sky is so blue
and so are your eyes?

You lie on a cloud of pillows
awaiting your tea.
I come to you with a smile and a cup.

You want to be with me, you say.
Today, like yesterday,
like every day for almost seven years.

I watch you sip, watch the clouds float across the sky.
I know what I want to do today.
I want to float across you like a cloud.

My Love Wants to Park

My love wants to park
in front of your house.

Thank God.
It's been driving me crazy
going around and around the block.

It's started breaking laws,
obsessively rolls through boulevard stops,
changes lanes without looking back.

It's taken over the transmission,
drops into second when I try to drive by
and rolls down its own windows.
I had to pull the horn wires
after it learned to "a-uugah"
at the sight of your address.

So just come out here please.
Please, just look under the hood
and kick the tires.

Try to stay away from the backseat.

In Praise of Breasts

occasioned by a photo of Da Chich Anan (The Paps of Anu)
County Kerry, Ireland

1

A camera focuses on the horizon
where two mounds swell
like breasts.

Oh, woman, when we make love
we hurry to the hills,
breathing in terrifying gasps
that shake the sky.

2

You come out of the shower,
water splashing, beading, spreading, dripping
as you bend to dry your legs.
Your breasts are what I see.
I take the sated towel
and throw it down,
bite your shoulder just enough
and watch your breasts rise
as you rise.

3

Lazy breasts in a cotton T-shirt,
they have forgiven me all my sins,
or so your eyes say
as you say "why don't you take me to lunch?"

4

You held your breasts in your hands
and talked about plastic surgery
but you meant
to be 17 again
before the babies came.
You could keep a man
with those breasts
and your 19th-century waist.

All I ever wanted
was your arms around my neck,
your breasts against me
wherever they fell
forever.

5.

Bless the steady surgeon
who by his work we know
loves breasts,
whose work left you whole
and beautiful,
who drew a fine line and said to Death,
you can't cross over here.

SYLLABLES

And somewhere,
inside the usual grammar
of morning,

between all the shortest syllables
of clock ring & water boil
egg tap & salt shake

you discover
you are
this body
that loves her

Even though
your finest words are gone,
leaving only the smallest bones
the metatarsals
the humble feet
of your love
to beat out their passions
on two rough heels

It happens here
over tea,
sun shoots one flawless arrow
across the tip of your spoon
and into hers
-the way she looks up

over the rim of her cup
one green eye,
then two

& suddenly
all four corners
of your world
meet here;
in the central moon
of your saucer

perfect alchemy

and it is then
that you swap
the ordinary floss
of morning
for a glimpse
of what the love
of this body
will be

Plum Poem

Taut
as a black plum
-would erupt
into a fountain
of pleasure
should the blunt knife
of our everyday passions
cut into

After Language

When all the drowsy metaphors
about women and fruit
have been peeled
and devoured;

there's just you, me
a bowl full of summer peaches,
two parentheses
with nothing in between
          (just space)
for the tongue's imagination

Marcie Hershman

MAKING LOVE TO ALICE

I imagine Gertrude making love to Alice
her generous and wise mouth upon her
breast her arms around hers the two
bodies fitting together, strangely
they are different and wonderfully they are
together. Gertrude being warm and full and
with Alice and Alice being warm and full with
Gertrude who is with her and the way
she is with her. Laughing. I imagine
they must know each other, the two, the one.

It is as with you and I. It is
with us as them. She then she and you then I
imagine. And in the act of imagining
make love to love to love to love

Karen Jastermsky

THE RIDE

My ten-speed is not a Harley 750 but I believe
it can be when she jumps on, wraps her hands

then arms around my waist, rests her chin
on my shoulder, and presses her breasts into

my back. October races across our faces as we
settle for Main Street instead of I-95. Today,

between classes, she whisked by in the hallway
and slipped me a piece of Dentyne. I caught

a whiff of her perfume, not the kind you spray
but dab. Riding now, I turn onto her road

and cut across the lawn. She unlocks the door
and leads me by the hand to her parents' bed,

parents away for the weekend, to the radio
on the night table playing "I've Got You Under

My Skin." As if Lewis and Clark, we're surveyors
of a new wilderness, when we slip off our jeans,

when our hands feel and fumble, when we hold
white breasts the way we cup water, when we

transform ourselves from naked girls
one minute into fallen women the next,

when we hear the unexpected BMW pulling
into the driveway, car doors slamming,

keys jiggling, feet climbing stairs,
the hand turning the bedroom doorknob.

Faye Dunaway at the Emmys, 1994

Not since I almost burned a hole through
the ironing board—that was when I got hot
around the collar by Dietrich in *Morocco*—

and not since *Bonnie & Clyde* or *Chinatown*
or *Network* or even *Mommie Dearest* have I ever
fallen for anyone, but last night I did.

Don't you know the moment I turned my head
to glance at the Emmys, there was Faye Dunaway
standing at the mike, looking stunning

in all-black, and when she said something
about how Hollywood has heart, I felt mine first
in my mouth then in my throat, then I rammed

into a wall, lost my footing, crashed downstairs
face first, and at the bottom, my shattered glasses.
"How did you break them?" the optometrist asks.

I tell him the honest-to-God truth, but he shakes
his head and rolls his eyes as if I had made up
not the story itself, but instead, Faye Dunaway.

Only Dream

I walk the late night streets
impervious to its dangers,
smell the coming rain pulling
smooth tensions of skin,
the fur of your eyes.
I gaze into a sky
speckled as some dark fowl's egg
and wish I were tucked with you
in haunted amber ritual,
spice and sacred wicks ablaze,
my lips plump against the small of your arms.
When with you I own the full bouquet of autumn,
finger the veins of leaves
watch their colossal collapse into
winter,
your breasts pour lava and steam
over me.
I cannot imagine withstanding
your pressed potency upon my hesitant, fitful core.
When with you something lost and timid starts to swell
as though stroked by your tongue
its curl and lash making me
unutterably mad.
I can only dream the sheer calypso of us,
the hard bronze stalks of our turning together.
For now,
I must only dream.

Unbridled

Only skinny girls give
their wedding dresses to Goodwill
I know
I've tried them on
watched people watching me
as I walked the aisle
to the dressing room
billowing with lace and tulle
polyester and beads
silk and satin
extravagance with armpit stains
nervous brides I guess

I went to find
one dress
to express my love to you
in drag
a lesbian with a veil and unbridled desire

I never came out
I couldn't even pull
them over my breasts
which you said this morning
were beautiful

Those dresses were designed
for women with
Tinkerbell waists

I couldn't help wondering
as you sucked my ampleness
if those marriages of starvation
lasted

We'll last
longer than satin
maybe not longer than polyester
(that's scary material)
What we have
fits
veil or no veil
dressed or naked
I love you
I do
I do

Willyce Kim

HomeComing

Glistening like the sea
your hair entwined
among my fingers
my mouth
your hair scattered
and black
like the strands
that sweep

across my shoulders
falling
and rising
my eyes cast back
heat for heat
wind rushes through the door
our skins are steaming
breath of my breath
first asian woman
I lay my head
upon your thigh
you are all the women
that I have ever feared
you are my mother
you are my mother's daughter
bone of my bone
throat arching
like a curve of the moon
you cry out my name
your mouth
a cave
a resting place
fills my tongue with song
flesh of my flesh
coming home to me
wet and sweet
in the morning light
your face
rises like mist
from the sea

my hair
bright
in the hollow
of your mouth
oh, blood of my blood.

Landscaping

Wild in the gathering
I fill my arms with your shoulders.
My mouth
leans into the ranges of your back
I tongue the ridges
turning them under like earth.
The ground heaves.
I dream I am planting rice.
Green onions dance between the fields
Your muscles swell beneath me
as koi swim the long curve of your spine.
I lap at your neck.
Rosemary spills from your hair.
While lightning flares across

darkened skies,

we ride your shoulders home.

Of love and guns in the wild wild West

Left-handed!
Like Billy the Kid!
She come along
one gloomy
Western day
and caught me
just-like-that
KA-BOOM!
with a bullet
to the heart
that I thought
I didn't have.

IT WAS GOOD

for sharon

it was good:
the plant by your bed
green with sunlight
while we made love   your face
melted into marble
delicate pink   liquid
with desire   and later
walking through
haphazard streets
the sky empty
my arm through yours
the shrubbery   holding back
its spring greenness   your despondency
the cruising police
the slits in the blinds
the striped sun across
your face   the plant
the wetness of your mouth

On your back you look like a scaled-down version
of the Maillol sculptures in the Tuileries,
or Moore's round-breasted women. I envision
losing myself in your body with such ease,
like spacing out in the dunes, sun-heated
curves, moist hollows, flooding you until
you dissolve, screaming, overcome with pleasure.
I've sworn to turn you over—I've a will
to match yours! We wrestle, I measure
my chances, and as usual you win,
and laughing I surrender undefeated.
Time to make the tea, allow some light in.
Reluctantly I let you let me go,
knowing we'll get there if we take it slow.

You look divine in drag: though I won't wear
skirts myself (too feminine) I love that smart
oyster-shade ensemble over white, your hair
coppery by contrast, and the sight
of your strong feet in pantyhose and two-
tone shoes excites me. Jacket on your shoulder,
you tell it to the judge while, getting bolder
by the minute, I fantasize what I'll do
to you after you've won your case
and I get you on a deserted beach somewhere
and pull those stockings off you. No disgrace
in playing with bygone traditions, is there?
The judge, bless her, sports a wig and a bow tie.
If I don't make you come this week, I'll die.

SOME UNSAID THINGS

I was not going to say
how you lay with me

nor where your hands went
& left their light impressions

nor whose face was white
as a splash of moonlight

nor who spilled the wine
nor whose blood stained the sheet

nor which one of us wept
to set the dark bed rocking

nor what you took me for
nor what I took you for

nor how your fingertips
in me were roots

light roots torn leaves put down—
nor what you tore from me

nor what confusion came
of our twin names

nor will I say whose body
opened, sucked, whispered

like the ocean, unbalancing
what had seemed a safe position

Breathing You In

The scent you say is no scent
rises from warm ports
between neck and shoulder.
Scent that isn't
witch hazel, vetiver, camphor,
lemon, but is just your skin,
raises a breeze on mine, unpredicted
as freshness I found in woods
where a few blond leaves hung from twigs.
Sweet sharpness,
scent of something still to come,
something soaked in—
chlorine on the cedar deck your thigh presses,
foot drifting in water,
eyes yellow amber behind closed lids.
Soaked in like sun
in the river whose cold silk
wrapped your body in August,
opened dark folds around you.
Closed, opened, around you.

RIGHT HERE, RIGHT NOW

Like a smile. Like her
frayed cuff brushing
the heel of her boot.
Like the metal fasteners of
her overalls. Like a
touch instead of a word.
Like the curve of a
downcast eyelid. Like her
beauty. Like the
weather. Like it or not, but I
do, I always do. Like
my laughter. Like my
desire. Like a hand
opening, unfurling. Like my
hand closing on her
wrist. Like affection. Like
attention. Like
paying attention, like
standing at attention.
Like a kiss. Like the kiss of
a slap.
Like a kiss.

What I Think of When You're Gone

I miss you.
Fresh baked bread. Blue collar.
Sweetness studded around you
like diamonds in jeans.
The way animals move near you, circling close.
The way you feed them each day, every day.
Without fail. The kitchen with your fingerprints
everywhere. Large, thick swirls that I lick
from the walls, the refrigerator door
my own body. I am an animal circling you
and the way you feed me could get us killed.
But each day, every day, you do it
without fail.

For us to love we must meet
danger between the sheets.
At work, walking down the street
buying shampoo, the Sunday paper
a bottle of water. I watch
your hands, strong as wheat
pull all the impossible moments together
into sunlight, into food.
I notice this with my life.
In the morning I stretch
spread my legs, take you in.
This is how I feed you. You smile.

Animals gather. Bread rises.
Tongues reach and gather
and reach again.

It is your birthday. In 45 years
no one has murdered you. Yet.
We celebrate. We practice safety
the way others practice the piano.
It is an art. We are masters.
We recite codes and tactics.
We measure threats and balance hatred.
Look for triumph and epiphany.
All this in a day. Every day.
Without fail.

I miss you. You are away for the weekend.
I feel a little afraid. It is not
car accidents or earthquakes I imagine.
It is violence. That bare and simple.
Even a short separation:
a run to the store, a weekend camping
could take you from me.
Someone could hate you in just the right amount
that day.

I, too have always been
a lesbian. *I have never been straight.*
But with you it is different. The hate
is more apparent. Urgent. Men stare at you,
challenge and spit. Even as you hold my hand
they flirt and proposition me. Women turn away

and whisper or stare without blinking.
They look at you and gasp. They parade
around you. A butch lesbian sideshow.
Danger splinters the air. From zero to ugliness
in seconds.

So when you return, come through the door
full of groceries and presents
it is a miracle. My heart rests as though
somehow in my sight, in my arms
I can protect you. If not that then
at least my love can touch all the places
in you they have hated. I say, *"I love you."*
You put one hand on the small of my back
one around my shoulders, pull me close.
You hold me this way, kiss me, slip
your hand under my shirt. My breasts
meet you taut and full.
You work your way down
press against my belly move the crotch
part of my underwear to one side.
I am slick and wet. You enter.
We are home.

Emily Lloyd

AT THE MICHIGAN WOMYN'S MUSIC FESTIVAL, 1994

(for Trish Moore)

brown skin, gold hair, green eyes:
you were the color of the woods you led me through
to the hammock some lovers had stretched
between two trees
and perhaps you'd been one of the lovers,
I didn't ask. My mother warned
her son about girls like you,

but you only wanted to talk. About your women:
one who was too attentive, one who ignored you.
I listened, but not too attentively, letting a daydream lazily rise
and settle into the haze between our bodies.
The hammock rocked us closer together, squashing it.
You lit each Camel impatiently,

as if it should have been lit the moment
a smoke occurred to you—lying in wait
for your warm lips. Rattled on
for an hour, ignoring me really,
but eventually you couldn't ignore

the hammock. Its shameless rhythm reminded you
of something. We kissed.

You're good, you said, surprised, but I wasn't
insulted. Girl,
I'd have waited all afternoon

to occur to you.

Audre Lorde

Woman

I dream of a place between your breasts
to build my house like a haven
where I plant crops
in your body
an endless harvest
where the commonest rock
is moonstone and ebony opal
giving milk to all of my hungers
and your night comes down upon me
like a nurturing rain.

Love Poem

Speak earth and bless me
with what is richest
make sky flow honey out of my hips
rigid as mountains
spread over a valley
carved out by the mouth of rain.

And I knew when I entered her   I was
high wind in her forest's hollow
fingers whispering sound
honey flowed   from the split cup
impaled on a lance of tongues
on the tips of her breasts   on her navel
and my breath   howling into her entrances
through lungs of pain.

Greedy as herring-gulls
or a child
I swing out   over the earth
over and over   again.

If It Happens During the Day

When the bombs hit will you be driving to work?
Will I have to climb onto the freeway
search every smelted steel box
until I find your hands?
I won't die right until I find your hands.

If I'm doing the shopping when it happens
I'd crawl through that smoldering swamp
past the mesh of wire racks, the truncated registers.
It won't matter that the money has blown all over,
the bodies of women pebbled with silver and glass.
It won't matter if my pants are bloody or my breasts exposed.
I'd hoist myself up once I reached concrete
and I'd know which direction would find you.

If this disaster drops like a wedge
into a day we can't undo,
and our bodies blaze up miles from each other,
it won't matter that the telephone has ruptured to bits,
power lines melting into pavement like crayon drawings.
It won't matter if we fought that morning.
I'd meet your gaze at that instant in spite of the distance.
I'd rise over this city like ash blown from a chimney,
and settle against you, and blot out the sun.

Insist the night is pulled snug around us
our stomachs together pressed into a psalm
the dark squared windows gleaming in their places
the cats asleep on either side.

TAKE ME WITH YOU NOW

please take my body
and take it with you as you go
          from earth to sun
and over these hills
mountains that rise above the clouds,
take me with you now

please take my body
mother, take me with you now
take me to the sea
into the salt ocean
deep into the waters where we began
take me with you now

please take my body
father, take me with you now
take me back to the prairie
golden fields & snow drifts deep
back to the plains where we both grew
take me with you now

please take my body
spirit, take me with you now
take me south, take me north
take me east, take me west
take me home to southern mountains
take me home to arctic seas
take me home to eastern woodlands
take me home on western winds

take me silently
take me fiercely
take me without words
        or hesitation
please take my body
lover,
take me with you now.

Touch

i might quiver under your touch
        if you should touch me
and the lights should go out
darkness a mystery, a warm blanket
enclosing our skin, wrapping our warm bodies
        in a halo of light.
glowing, pulsating, then
        flashing and flashing and finally exploding
bodies like shooting stars
glowing thru the darkness
leaving traces of our magic in the sky
        a rainbow touching earth

Lynn Martin

THE HAIRCUT

And so you decided to change.
Locust trees gnarled over you,
the green buds only a promise
but one you took seriously
enough to point a toe
and consider the possibility of dance
as each bone awakened
to its fifty-fifth spring.

You have capped your head,
shorn of the responsible hair
touching your shoulders
in a straight lined, no nonsense way.
Now you are all light, each strand
lifting you from the ordinary ground
to shine like some just imagined story
about to take wing.

My fingers smooth the grass beneath me,
silky and cool as a remembered
flight down the length of your leg.
"We can't be in our fifties," you say
brushing silver from your eyes.
Without a word I reach for you,
feathers and wings and everything
suddenly alive.

Rainy Day

Rain has silvered your hair
until each strand clings to the pillow
damp and slippery with light.

The skylight over our head
echoes the melody
of my body touching you,
alive with the downpour
we know as love.

I am the rain in your arms, murmuring
and forever falling.
You are silent as any animal
intent on living and finding its way
while I must give voice
to the mists which surround us,
transport us to the very source
of all this sound soundlessly
caressing my ear, the inside of my palm.

Our bodies are an echo of each other,
familiar, like the same deer
glimpsed every morning at sunrise,
known but without form.

I collect buckets of water
to pour at your feet.
Curled around you, I talk to the rain.
You answer with my name.

My Old Lover

My old lover and I
went fishing.
We believed enough years had passed
since the breakup,
that time had pulled us so far apart,
that we could just
go fishing.

My old lover taught me
how to fish, all those years ago.
We were young and in lust
and I was willing to follow her
to that hot, boring, mosquito-infested
pond and learn to fish,
because she wanted me to.

In time, I learned to love
to fish.
After we separated, I kept fishing.
I took all my other lovers fishing.
Some learned to fish, some even liked it
but none ever loved to fish like
my old lover.

So, when my old lover and I met again,
after all those years,
we decided to go fishing.

But it was different this time.
Now we shared the love of the water,
the love of fishing, and the maturity
that the years had given us.

The sun was still stifling hot, but
it wasn't angry anymore because
my old lover shielded the glare by
reading me poetry on the bank of that
fishless river in the long afternoon.

Then, we went fishing in the midnight.
My old lover introduced me to
glow-in-the-dark bobbers.
We sat on the dock, on the lake
in the moonlight and watched our
green and red pin-lights bob
up and down on the soft waves.

My old lover called me to her side
and showed me the sparkling path
of the moonlight on the water.
It looked as if bubbles of light
were floating up from the bottom
of the lake and popping in a burst
of white on the tips of the waves.

My old lover and I were fishing.
But in that dreamy midnight,
we stood mesmerized on the dock
on the lake in the raining starlight.
Quietly, without intending to,

we shared the poetry of our lives.
Silently, without meaning to,
my old lover and I
loved again.

Judith McDaniel

Body of Love

I.

Entre la muerte y yo
he erigido tu cuerpo . . .
Rosario Castellanos

Because from the beginning you were fated
to be mine, because in the years before now,
apart, we learned the dance's movements, because
during these last long days I had stopped hoping,
but never ceased yearning, we came together
like the ocean meets a high cliff-crescendo
of foam on dark still waters beneath—and you
rest in my arms, a rock splashed by jubilant
waters.

Body of love, of lust, earthbound joy, festival
of taste, feast of smell, I burrow between
forked roots, wander with languid fingers
through crevices, at times a quiet stream
sliding, though not unnoticed, into your earth's

warm cave, at times the wild full river breaking
over banks of containment, flooding the swollen
plains, leaping from quiescence into the dangerous
unknown.

We know the spirit through these bodies, learn
ourselves by taste and smell, touch our inner-
most souls with hands and tongues, exchange
permissions to be known—to allow another body
access, most holy terror, most longed for
and most feared—because of this,
this confirmation:
that I know myself immortal by the weight
of your earth on my chest.

II.

Incomplete people, that's what he called us,
those of us who love our own image in another.
The only whole love, the only love God approves,
is between men and women. Nature intended—
he pauses, searching for the image—*physical*
complement between men and women, that is missing—
he still gropes for words.

It ought to give us pause,
this weighty disapproval from one who says he knows
what God and Nature mean.

But I know my own nature.   Listen:

They call it love-making, what has happened
between the two people lying now in damp sleep
oblivious to the August sun high above the whispering
pines outside their bedroom window. Making love.
The whispered urgent yes, the look deep behind the eyes,
the opening,
breathless waiting for a touch that lingers everywhere
but there, there where she is waiting for more than fingers
lightly brushing back and forth, waiting for the smooth
silky warm first tongue touch. How is this love? This passion
that slides these two over the edge of self into a deep well
where they sink down and down, forgetting who is she and
who is she, forgetting time, that fiction which folds people
out of self, this effortless joining, this merging of tongues
and fluids, soft sighs, urgent cries? Could this make
love? Listen: Their hearts
have been changed by what has transpired, this breathing
into one another's souls started something growing,
something new that wasn't here before—a deepening,
some attitude, perhaps, which allows each to notice each
with a careful attention, with a joy that opens, opens,
letting in the sun.

Christian McEwen

AND SUNDAY MORNING

All day in a daze of your making
of our making   love making
all day awake   to the sleep   of the ship
of the under-cover lover   the above-board sprawl
all day in the daze   of the laze   of us both
in the puckered nipple   and the salt expanse
all day in the thigh   in the sly eye
of the belly-button   in the curve of your flank
in the laughing mustache of my own pubic hair
all day in the nimbus   the haze
in the cloud of the sound of the mosquito buzz
of our love

Mary Ann McFadden

MARRIAGE

I

I wake up and turn and put my forehead in the place
        between your breasts, nothing so safe,
Soft, nothing so fine and warm skin underneath the shirt
        you have on.

You let me stay, god bless me, breathing dark and long
        as the morning minutes turn, and then

As I wake and stretch free, you burrow in with your face
and hands, finding me,
Running your practiced fingers around and around.

I curl for you, my girl, my lips above and below
start their swell,
And then we tell our dreams and argue awhile over who
hogged the sheets,
Who snored, who slept least, the purl and knit of our
sweet-tart, part-whole

Sickness-and-health waking up together. If I hadn't
pretended to be asleep,
You'd have chatted all night, I know, my gray mare,
my duck, my grumbler.

Time to go to work. The hot pink underpants I gave you
for a joke
Go yanking up your thighs and over your rump as you
complain and pout.

Oh! How I ill-treat you, my prize, my little sauerkraut.

II

Something is pulling you up out of our Saturday morning
and into the world of your mind,
That brute machine with its hard lips and thighs, eyes
that see not me, not my flesh, my bones,

Not the fact that I'm dying. You're not curious but tolerant
as you rise and grind
And bring me a cup to wake me. You're far out in the day,
the near year,

Already running hard, numbers flipping like pennies' worth
of gasoline. I want you to go.
I want you to zoom over your bright horizon, my jellybean.

But give me full five fathoms first, my fist, my submarine,
give me a smack, a shine.

III

The great barge of you beached on my side of the bed,
refusing to move over, Lover, dammit,

It's my turn to sleep in. I like your company but sometimes
I swear . . .

Like today when the first words I hear are angry words,
something you dreamed about your mother
Only she was me and anyway, there there, I'm sure you had
a perfect right to wake up bothered.

All I want is a little space. The world's going to hell and I'm
getting older. We never know.
You're lying there solid as the hills and I'm trying to turn
in my narrow row, and then the clock ticks once.

Sweetheart, I want you here. But sometimes I want you
smaller, quieter, nicer, mousier.
I want you in my pocket, Dear, though I suppose I'm being
unreasonable. It happens, but it's rare.

IV

Mazatlán, Mexico

All those years of hiding what you feel, protestant years
learning to keep control,
And now I want you to peel and weep and surge and crawl
and beg for more,
Not proud, not tall and pressed and ironed and showered
and shined, but small

And helpless once in a while. You can be a baby.

I want you generous and shrill, full of womanly feeling,
fishwife and all, those wide thighs
High as the hills, the very grass groaning as it grows,
breaking in its needy silky sigh.

I feel so far away. Write me, but make the paper wet,
I want sweat and shit and fingernails
And hair, wildflowers and slime folded up together,
wildlife, not tame toast and tea.

Lover, I'm alone here in paradise, alone and queer
and greedy.

V

I want you to take me back, now that I'm back, now
that I'm here, and you do, you are.
You seem to have forgiven me for the little things
that wear and tear,

You've taken me in to your self like a bad brother,
 not denying that I irritate,

My famous, difficult girl, you've breathed me in
 like a temper, slept with me
While my knots and whorls worked loose and I mourned
 the empty spaces,
Washed me with water and oil like the feet of Christ
 or a wood floor.

How can I fail? I had always thought that if I fell
 I would be ridiculed,
Or left in my puddle. But when I goof up you love me more
 because I need it more.

If I had the art to say this new I'd start a religion, or a war.

VI

Sometimes it grows tedious. I'm pissed because you push
me away, not flirtatious, not crisp but limp lettuce,
lukewarm tea. "Is it age?" I wonder, "Is it me?"
Or is this the fate of the too-long together? We become
like sisters, like mother-daughter, like old maid friends
squabbling equitably over coffee, coughing up phlegm,
suffering flu diarrhea, and then when I see you naked:
nothing. Less than nothing. A chill reminds me
we're growing more frail, that the end, though not soon,
is just over the hill. Not the end of us together,
but of fascination, of rolling wild on the floor. Did we ever?
Or was it just a dream I thought we shared: two mild-
mannered ordinary women turning to sweet beasts in bed.

What was your dream? Two lesbians knitting, cooking?
Christ, you make me so mad.

VII

Sometimes it comes down to this: companionship,

and the way we touch, not urgent so much as sensuous,
the way we scratch each other's back and say
it's better than sex, almost, has to be enough, and is

somehow, though it might not be if it were all there was.

So much I want to say about love, and yet I stanch the urge
to gush, the way I bank the coals in the wood stove,
or the way I rake up piles of leaves and leave them
to smolder, almost smother the small fire underneath,
and allow the burn to slowly fill the yard, the whole day,

the whole life if I'm lucky.

We touch for comfort and pleasure and yes it's still there,
not the need to snatch and tear but the underground
warm waters of eternal measure, the source

in which we bathe, and of which we drink at our leisure.

VIII

Warm blood and warm water rushing through the rivers
    of your body to your fingertips,
To your toes, coursing down the sweeps of thighs
    and calves, or wide

As your wrists, your spread hands and on into the day,
    you warm the sheets, the room,
My side of the bed, you warm the water in the tub
    where I bathe after you like a pup,

Like a dog adoring. And like a dog I lick you up, my food
    my god, my green pastures,
The way you throw back your head, pretend you're tied
    and let me have you, pried,
Unslung, disjointed and hung out in the sun, my vegetarian,
    but nevermind.

The spring comes from you, you tricky fool
    pointing to the daffodils
As if you didn't know perfectly well what you'd done

    With your arms sprawled
And your breasts swung low and your drawl.

Skin
on skin
Pale cool
flesh
heats
up
under
my lips
Flushes a
deep pink
and gleams
with moisture
there

You moan a soft
throaty
sound
I tremble with
your
need
your breath quickens

There There
There Yes
There
Oh
This
is what
I live for

Jane Miller

THE HEALING FOUNTAINS

My last unnatural day began
on top of somebody, loosely speaking,

who was screaming about the dark times.
I realized that whether you pose Rose, or Rose poses,

it's prose.
So I finally said to myself, that's not a life, that's a dancefloor,

and those aren't lips, you asshole, that's *lipstick.*
The flesh itself,

it's not exact, it's precise,
skin and blood,

that thundercloud whose lightning pierced my soul.
That fake schedule of the future, too full of Fridays,

had the fish hopping mad about it.
All the while working love with a migraine,

they nonetheless swam, just an option, not a destiny,
toward the healing fountains

because they cared, not for me,
but for the woman I would become,

and all their large, magnified underwater bodies
never spoke, of course,

but had the right language bent out of shape
so I finally heard

you tell me you love me, in my ear like
on the phone because I couldn't see you.

There was never a home, with my old lovers in midair it was
different finally to find their place in the sun,

as you said, Lord Jesus of Nazareth,
completing another action. Which reminds me,

I appreciate that you are more
than halfway done

with the creation of the world, because now that we are closer
to forever, the poem has enough time

to demand the sequence cast aside.
In other words it's a shock

to love someone else entirely.

New Body

There's a sort of eternity
when we're in bed together
whether silently you awaken
me with the flat of your hand
or sleep breathing with a small scratch
in your throat, or quietly attach
a bird to the sky I dream
as a way in to my body—

Now you have made me excited
to accept heaven as an idea
inside us, perpetual
waters, because you let yourself
fall from a sky you invented
to a sea I vaulted
when it was small rain
accumulating—My heart drained

there and fills now in time
to sketch in the entire
desert landscape we remember
as an ocean port,
that part of me accepting
your trust, a deep
voluptuous thrust into my hours,
that has no earthly power

but lives believing you were made for me
to give in to completely,
every entry into you the lip

of water that is in itself scant hope
broken into like sleep
by kisses—Policed in the desert
by a shooting star, we are the subversive
love scratched out of sky, o my visitor.

Patricia Monaghan

THE GODDESS POMONA SINGS TO THE OLD WOMAN

You stood there,
a splendid autumn tree,

your trunk so firm
and strong, your hair

a radiance of flame,
your limbs brushed red,

and all I could think
was how strong the sap

pulsed in you, strong
as spring, all I could

think was how deep
you went, all that

rich sap in you,
deeper and deeper and

deeper and how I wanted
to pull your limbs down

to me then, there, under
the open sky, and how

I wanted you then,
there, to flame up

at my touch, how
I wanted to fall

burning, burning, burning,
and ignite all the hills

in a ring of bright flame
around you, old tree,

old splendid woman,
old treasure, old heart.

How I wanted you then.
How I'm wanting you now.

Diana to Her Maiden

No, sapling, no, I cannot climb
you yet, you bend in each
breeze like a flame in wind,

it is too soon, too soon.
Next year we will go
hunting under the half moon

and fall, damp and breathless
on soft moss near a stream,
and I will sing yes, yes,

the time and you are ripe, sapling,
little tree, and I will climb,
then, climb your brown limbs

and we will be all sugared
from the sap of you then,
the two of us tangled, ungirded,

unguarded, unblushing, unbound.
Oh, girl, your soft limbs . . .
Go, go call the hounds.

Honor Moore

SHENANDOAH

Photograph: Breakfast after our first full night:
Elbow on the table, fist against your face, intent
        on the cup you look into. Your hair glints
            in three-year-old light.
In these rooms of borrowed furniture, white
walls, wide windows that curve, I have been solitary.
        A cymbedium orchid. Artichokes. Fresh
            trout. I tear pink netting from
the orchid, float it. Red wine is breathing. A plane
lands hours away, and I can think of you driving
        a valley roofed with clouds, your voice
            like the charge of new weather.

Yesterday, eyes shut, sun on my face, I could
remember you viscerally: Heat, sun that caressed
        our naked skin, blond grasses, weeds baked
            to vivid rust. There was no

snow—odd that far north in late October. From ours
other mountains were feathery with bare trees
    and some phenomenon of light turned
        their billowing crests
lavender. See those mountains make a giant sprawled
on her back: those, breasts; the one called Otter, torso.
  See the lake bright near her cheek, the
        trout stream etch her chin.

I am afraid in the vestibule, your face
smiling its guileless welcome. I want to cry, hold you,
    open through your breasts into safe billowing
        darkness. I kiss you
as if we are just friends. I lead you through
white rooms. I hand you the orchid because I cannot
    tell you. You reach. I start, as if your touch were
        too much light, I trim
the artichokes. The red wine breathes. I must cover
the curved windows. In this valley roofed with clouds, I live
    alone in rooms on a street where
        all the shades are pulled.

We drink red wine. We unbutton, touch. We eat
trout—clouded eye, clear black night shut from the house,
    petal
    flush of your skin. We eat artichokes, mark
        leaf after leaf with our teeth.
The orchid floats. It is your darkness I want with my
mouth. If I could speak as sound not edged into
    word, I could tell you. Leaves now: two, four,
        five at once. We reach

center, loose lavender-streaked swirl, split the naked
heart in the night bed where I speak with my hands
and we breathe, mouth to mouth, unedged,
shorn to simple tenderness.

Cherríe Moraga

LOVING IN THE WAR YEARS

Loving you is like living
in the war years.
I *do* think of Bogart & Bergman
not clear who's who
but still singin a long smoky
mood into the piano bar
drinks straight up
the last bottle in the house
while bombs split
outside, a broken
world.

A world war going on
but you and I still insisting
in each our own heads
still thinkin how
if I could only make some contact
with that woman across the keyboard
we size each other up
yes . . .

Loving you has this kind of desperation
to it, like do or die, I
having eyed you from the first
time you made the decision to move
from your stool
to live dangerously.

All on the hunch
that in our exchange of photos
of old girlfriends, names
of cities and memories
back in the states
the fronts we've manned
out here on the continent
all this on the hunch

that *this* time there'll be
no need for resistance.

Loving in the war years
calls for this kind of risking
without a home to call our own
I've got to take you as you come
to me, each time like a stranger
all over again. Not knowing
what deaths you saw today

I've got to take you
as you come, battle bruised
refusing our enemy, fear.

We're all we've got. You and I

maintaining
this war time morality
where being queer
and female is as rude
as we can get.

If

If in the long run
we weep together
hold each other
wipe the other's mouth
dry from the kiss pressed there
to seal the touch
of spirits separated
by something as necessary
as time,
we will have done enough.

DAMN YOU, LADY

(The Funky Double Sonnet Tragicomic Lesbian Feminist Blues)

Damn you, lady, get out of my blood for good.
Your eyes, hair, laugh, your politics—erase
them—how your body's swift lewd grace once stood
beside me, how love lit your falcon face.

> Damn you, lady, I refuse to wail
> one moment longer so uncritically
> over you—as if I were a fool
> (or even incorrect politically).

Your gestures in quickliquid flow,
your voice, indigo as a violin's—
get out. Go, let my dreams sleep free
of you, your fragrance, words, songs, silences . . .

> Lovesick morons fail the revolution,
> mooning about while work needs to be done
> and feminism's surely the solution
> to everything—except your being gone.

. . . the way you slept, woke, moved at midnight,
your antic grin that struck and blazed me glad
to be alive, the way you loved a fight
in a just cause. The way you drove me mad.

Damn you, lady, I will not obsess
one second more. Love's just a masquerade
at which we women, like men, can oppress
(an awkward truth we'd rather not parade).

but see I have regained myself entire,
immune to you, asbestos to your fire.

Damn you, lady, I will yet live through
this memory, everywhere I turn, of you.

Bonnie Morris

Loving You Has Become a Political Act

I want to start at the top of your head & work my way down to the arch of your feet. I want to place one hand on the back of your neck and one hand between your breasts and slowly feel the pulses between our skins. I want to lower you very gently onto a firm soft surface, bed, beach, field, rug & look at you for hours & hours. I want your fingers on my arm. I want you absolutely. Tell me that you want me. I want to eat out of the light in your eyes & drink out of the white in your teeth. I want to feel you kissing me deeply all around me, the crown of my head, the palms of my hands, the insides of my knees. Tell me that you love me. Brush your fingers through my hair. I want to kiss you from your throat to your forehead & listen in the still room for the sounds of those good kisses. I want to feel you break into a hot sweat. I want your hard bicep under my hand. I will lean over & kiss you & you will flush with arousal & pull me down alongside you. Then we will entwine our sound limbs & strong hands & exchange our tongues for twenty-seven minutes. I will part your lips & hear you sigh. Slide down me like an arrow. Feel the ocean burn between our legs. Outside there is a desert, night, a small town, bare beach, city park, back yard, dark sky, winter. Press your mouth against my neck. Kiss me so the flesh of our mouths meets & our noses touch. Pull back & look at me. Trace your fingers along my skin. Give me chills. Make me shudder. Sing to me. Pull my hair very very very gently letting it slide through your long fingers. Brush yourself against me like a cat. Now I say, now curl into my beating heart.

Nicola Morris

A Partial Eclipse

I want to suck your nipples
first one and then the other
but your left breast is stitched
with black thread.

The sunlight will not reach
that nipple, not even when you garden
with no shirt, the first spring day
clumps of ice clinging to grass
in the northern shadows.

Yesterday you told me you didn't want
me to touch your left side
from your hip to your breast.

The top of my leg is fine
you said as my hand passed
the rich ridge where your thigh
slips into your hip . . .

What is hidden, love?
Describe the colors
rushing towards you
when your body is taken over
your fury not yet molded neatly
into words, your love
not yet ready for me.

Thérèse Murdza

EATING SZECHUAN EGGPLANT

like sucking up along your collar bone
and licking heat,
the ink
of your tattoos.

with you
i've eaten roses,
red and full and fragrant,
put them whole inside me,
swallowed and felt
their skin slide
into my body
and bloom.

Eileen Myles

I always put my pussy
in the middle of trees
like a waterfall
like a doorway to God
like a flock of birds.
I always put my lover's cunt
on the crest
of a wave
like a flag
that I can
pledge my
allegiance
to. This is my
country. Here,
when we're alone
in public.

My lover's pussy
is a badge
is a night stick
is a helmet
is a deer's face
is a handful
of flowers
is a waterfall
is a river
of blood
is a bible
is a hurricane
is a soothsayer.
My lover's pussy
is a battle cry
is a prayer
is lunch
is wealthy
is happy
is on teevee
has a sense of humor
has a career
has a cup of coffee
goes to work
meditates
is always alone
knows my face
knows my tongue
knows my hands
is an alarmist
has lousy manners
knows her mind

I always put
my pussy in the middle
of trees
like a waterfall
a piece of jewelry
that I wear
on my chest
like a badge
in America
so my lover & I
can be safe.

Lesléa Newman

NOTHING LIKE IT

ain't nothing like
a handsome butch
standing at my door
all spiffed up
in a fresh pressed shirt
pleated pants
snappy shoes
a long stemmed red rose
in one hand
my heart
in the other

Night on the Town

When I step into my red silk panties and swivel into
the strapless bra my butch bought me for Valentine's Day

When I slide on my black mesh stockings with toes pointed,
sitting on the bed like some Hollywood movie queen

When I shimmy into my spandex dress that sparkles
over the tops of my thighs: a disco ball over a snappy crowd

When I puff on my pink clouds of blush, brush my eyelashes
long and lush, smear my lips and nails richer than ruby red

When I step into my sky high heels, snap on some earrings
and slip seventeen silver bracelets halfway up my arm

When I dab my shoulders and neck, earlobes and wrists,
cleavage and thighs with thick, musky perfume

When I curl my hair into ringlets that dip over one eye
and bounce off my shoulder like a Clairol girl gone wild

When I turn from the mirror, pick up my purse
and announce to my butch that I'm ready to go

When I see her kick the door shut, hear her
declare, "We're not going anywhere, tonight,"

When I whine and say, "But we never go out,"
following her back to the bedroom, my lips in a pout

When I give in and let her have her way
with me pretending that wasn't my plan all along

What My Butch Would Say

"I'm a breast man" but
she's got manners
won't talk with
her mouth
full

Barbara Noda

Her Ruby Lips Like Biting into a Strawberry

strawberries   strawberries   strawberries
it seems I have been writing about
    strawberries forever
how she glistens in the morning fog
between the warm breasts of soil
    crawling with life
I whisper the name of Strawberry
her cool mystery like a homemade wine
    secretly born in my cellar
she bathes herself in the afternoon light
as fresh as a bunch of crimson dahlias
    her green stems vibrating
    from the translucent vase on your kitchen table

beware of strawberries
she is the poison oak scampering the fields
  her red-tinged leaves
  dare to be fondled
oh! strawberries forever!
I have been writing about
strawberries for as long as I remember
  and I was suckled
  on their sweet and wild taste

Karen Lee Osborne

CHEST PAINS

for J.

Two nights ago you woke
to chest pains and a sudden fear.
Now you are brushing your teeth
with your right hand, angry
because you dislike
being clumsy. The IV
crawls from under a wide band
of clear tape smeared with blood,
rises from your left hand,
glucose that helps
not at all and forces
you up every hour to pee.

A neon green snake
fuels your nose while white
circles kiss your breasts,
anchoring the gray talons
feeding signals to a blue box.

You spit mouthwash
into a pink dish
and flop back
like a limp doll,
telling me your hair
is so oily you'll
wake up to pimples
sprouting from your scalp.

I return with shampoo,
then scrub my hands
clean as a surgeon's.
I cover your shoulders with
white towels and then
wash your hair without water.

The white lather rises,
sea foam murmuring
as tiny bubbles break. I
massage your scalp
with the tenderness of a wolf
who will not give in
to hunger. I take
my time. Here in your hair

I am feeling my way
to the bone. Touching
the hidden skin, my
fingers relax, my arms,
my nerves. Our breathing slows.

When your eyes close
I dry you gently, comb
out your hair, long as my breath,
and dry you again.

Now I watch you, remembering
how it was to hold you, knowing
I will not kiss you tonight.
I wonder what the blue box
knows of your heart, what
messages the wires convey.
How our desire has spared us,
how we have lived without
knowledge, the dark wings
of fear unseen in our night.

TRAIN

I am forever holding my peace
at the back of some church,
my tongue stayed by the dark wave
of hair between your ivory shoulders.
You are sixteen, at the altar,
a daughter of steel.

I hear a train pulling earth.
The iron in our veins
goes to an open hold in the harbor,
to a steel mill for use in the trades.
Its roar, the wheels of the earth
braking at morning light

at a blue bruise,
at the nights you spent calling God
from the backseat of a car.
Your father with his problem heart
could have been the captain
of this industry, he gave

you away a long time ago.
The struggle of our girlhood
was the body.
Yours, mine and theirs.
Once you and I cut our thumbs
in the woods, mixed our blood.

Now yours courses along this aisle
and mine courses back to the sun
setting on the tracks, on how we balanced
and ran along the rails, then hid
when the train came bearing down.
We smoked burning green leaves,

made many vows.
Now I'd say, most of our lives
have been forged.
Back then when you opened the gifts
of frying pans and toasters and irons and cash,
did you look for mine?

I'm sending it now
with a full head of steam
blowing its lonely whistle
on the silver tracks back
to my arms.
Take it. Untie the strings

of memory and desire
and open this forgotten cargo.
Let love overtake you like a rage.

Journey

the track of time loses
itself inside your sleeve
as you slip from your shirt

arrivals and departures
vanish like shadow
between your breasts

along your thighs
my hand slows
over curves

everything has been given
wheels my palms
roll along the smooth rails

of your bones
putting you almost to sleep
my tongue bridges

the ravines
and the isolated roads connect
like my fingertips

at your windows
where the countryside
opens its dreams to our berth

we ride the stream
miles and miles
of day following night

effortless even with our freight
enroute with our hearts'
motion

H. Emilia Paredes

Breath #11

The curve of your breasts
          by sunrise
and sound of snow geese
          in migration.

Maybe it is flight we crave, or soaring, gliding
          or melting.
Through soundless night I hover
lines of solitary battles etched
on my wrists, throat arched
as you preen the fluttering thing between
          my thighs.

You like my lusts, my agonies
wind whistling through hollow bones
          your skin beneath my fingernails
transfiguring the distance between body and earth.

You are wings of smoke, of flame
inside me, vein and artery
sweat and terror
flying.

For an instant, I am clouds crossing
the sky of your spine
from the edge of your gaze, I watch the wings
of your eyelids, open shut   open shut

Breath #14

You juggle the fire rings of Saturn, a universe
spins, whirls, plummets, glows light years after
your touch. The sky is troubled. On the fence outside
morning glories wilt to sleep, shudder in translucent dreams

by dawn white and violet petals open
in our eyes, forgetfulness.
You are a stranger to me
the cosmos stranger still.

Let me recognize you in the glimmer of the hundreth star
which fell the day you were born
pungent scent of your skin
curtains stir, lace and filigree, a woman's silhouette
the topography of desire.

In the yard, crickets hush.
In this moment like candle flame
    only I witness the life of your body
    temporal, a meteor
    our bodies extinguished

one inside the other, angels watch
    whisper love and nothing
I shrill, you answer until I fall, infinite particles
    from your eyes.

You bring me pristine worlds
    fragrance and colors
    wind across damp flesh
I bite soft, then hard joy, leaving dark red-blue roses.

I give you my flowering self
    star jasmine, winter rose, morning glory
    and the restlessness of luminaries on a clear
        summer's night.

Pat Parker

1

My lover is a woman
  & when i hold her -
    feel her warmth -
    i feel good - feel safe

Then/ i never think of
my families' voices -
never hear my sisters say -
bulldaggers, queers, funny -
come see us, but don't
bring your friends -
it's okay with us,
but don't tell mama
it'd break her heart
never feel my father
turn in his grave
never hear my mother cry
Lord, what kind of child is this?

2

My lover's hair is blonde
& when it rubs across my face
it feels soft -
feels like a thousand fingers
touch my skin & hold me
and i feel good.

Then/ i never think of the little boy
who spat & called me nigger
never think of the policemen
who kicked my body and said crawl
never think of Black bodies
hanging in trees or filled
with bullet holes
never hear my sisters say

white folks hair stinks
don't trust any of them
never feel my father
turn in his grave
never hear my mother talk
of her back ache after scrubbing floors
never hear her cry -
Lord, what kind of child is this?

3

My lover's eyes are blue
& when she looks at me
i float in a warm lake
  feel my muscles go weak with want
    feel good - feel safe

Then/ i never think of the blue
  eyes that have glared at me -
  moved three stools away from me
    in a bar
  never hear my sisters rage
  of syphilitic Black men as
    guinea pigs -
  rage of sterilized children -
  watch them just stop in an
  intersection to scare *the old*
    white bitch.

never feel my father turn
  in his grave
never remember my mother
teaching me the yes sirs & mams
  to keep me alive -
never hear my mother cry,
Lord, what kind of child is this?

4

And when we go to a gay bar
  & my people shun me because i crossed
    the line
  & her people look to see what's
  wrong with her - what defect
  drove her to me -

And when we walk the streets
  of this city - forget and touch
  or hold hands and the people
  stare, glare, frown, & taunt
  at those queers -

I remember -
  Every word taught me
  Every word said to me
  Every deed done to me
  & then I hate -
  i look at my lover
  & for an instance - doubt -

Then/ i hold her hand tighter
And i can hear my mother cry.
Lord, what kind of child is this.

Gerry Gomez Pearlberg

SAILOR

The girls go by in their sailor suits
They catch my eye in their sailor suits
Big or slight they all grin like brutes
In steam-ironed pants and buffed jet boots
They saunter right up my alley.

I study their easy, confident strides
Crew cuts and white hats capping decadent eyes
They shiver the pearl on night's oystery prize
They shiver me timbers, unbuckle me thighs
This alley was made for seething.

From the sweat of the street lamp or lap of the sea
A smooth sailor girl comes swimming to me
Says she wants it right now and she wants it for free
Clamps her palms to my shoulders, her knees to my knees
This alley was made for cruising.

Her face is dark coffee, her head has no hair
Her cap shines like neon in the bristling night air
She pins her brass metals to my black brassiere
Tucks her teeth like bright trophies behind my left ear
This alley is very rewarding.

She tosses her jacket and rolls up her sleeves
On her arm's a tattoo of an anchor at sea
She points to the anchor and whispers "That's me."
And the wetter I get the more clearly I see
This alley was made for submersion.

Her fingers unbutton my 501's
This girl's fishing for trouble and for troubling fun
She slides off her gold rings and they glint like the sun
Then she smirks, rubs her knuckles, and spits out her gum
This alley was made for swooning.

Now she's pushing her prow on my ocean's sponge wall
Uncorking my barnacle, breaking my fall
And there's pink champagne fizzling down my decks and
  my hall
As she wrecks her great ship on my bright port-of-call
This alley was made for drowning.

Meredith Pond

Velocity

There is more than speed to this moment, this you,
this love without fear of time that hasn't passed,
no month yet, no season, no year. We hold fast
inside this moment and kiss towards forever
and the moon through willows as fire dances
across our mattress licking wood to embers

and you burn against me, smolder, singe me
rough with your scratches or smooth with the palm
of your hand, your hair a tumble of roaming shadow
on my belly as you fuck me until I beg you to stop,
because I know, I know, I am way past midnight,
way past coming, or wanting to, my body
disappearing like sugar in your tea, jasmine
in your mouth, at the nape of your neck, between
your breasts, your heart drumming like my tongue
deep inside you, like your hand deep inside me, rocking,
through this waveborne night that once knew only terror
and the ancient rage of women who somehow knew they
needed, wanted, had to have more than the world of men
could ever offer.

Deidre Pope

LULLABY

Commitment is boring. So we're told.
Our love will fade like sunworn curtains
and it'll be youandme youandme: same old.

True, we don't spend weekends in bed anymore,
or tackle each morning on three hours sleep.
These days we curl around midnight for

talk that happens only when defenses fall by
the bedside and sleepiness opens us up.
There is something to be said for a lullaby

of touch, familiar hands and voice
that cross us safely over from conscious
to closed. It is hard-won, this choice

to refuse the fairy tale, the hourly kiss-
turns-to-kiss-turns-to-a-shrugging-
of-covers. We know the impossibility of exist-

ing in such perpetual bliss; inconvenient mask
that cracks open into long and violent nights.
From storybook to here is a movement, not a fast

change backstage. It is a pencil scratching
two circles out of one closed disk. It is breath -
a long, slow stretch toward relinquishing.

Desire

clit
breasts
lips legs luscious
ass

separating the parts is not a feminist thing to do

curve of ankle
fingertips

but the way you look in jeans
is not the way you look in nothing
but my shirt

and the way I breathe
when you flick my nipple with your tongue
is not the way I breathe
when your hand is inside
me like a nested bird

cunt   throat   middle finger   breast-bone

if one thing leads to another
then I begin with your hair
your eyes   followed by
your mouth
long neck
and there I'm unbuttoning your shirt
and will itemize
every inch of you
with my hot tongue greedy fingers my
whole body (which is nothing
other than its parts) calculating the sum
of yours

A Hum To Say I'm Missing Your Touch

to Paula

Water breaking from rocks. Finally
a sound to undo the drum of crickets
pushing summer to its limit.
This green slide on my skin, this sound
I straddle, water on water
on rocks filled with light like the light
inside me when you un-buckle my limbs with your
lips breathing air into me until I float
in your hands the way I float now down
this river, swimming, you singing your way
into me, swimming, singing, making my body
outgrow its house of bone, its breath of air,
its hard tales it likes to tell.
This sound finally larger than the sound
of trucks passing by the river, larger
than the voices of children playing
at the water's edge, larger than the patience
of mothers watching those children play, as large
as the hum you set thrumming when you tongue this
nest of hair making my skin swell from the wet V
of my thighs held here now above the water
slipping through rocks singing this thrum,
this hum remembered in your name.

Amanda Powell

Aubade

1.

For the first time
she wakes on both sides of my dream.

2.

Conversation was all I thought
lacking, good talk—

then call her and talk,
I told myself—while

insistent and differing opinions were heard
from my breasts, ribs, knees,
etc.

3.

No crack in the parched earth,
no dry fork in a fallen branch, this

is where I stretched on lapped rocks
as a child; barnacles clung nearby;
I touched the reticent lips of snails,
squeezed seaweed pods,
stroked through
that salt:

and one hand now
finds her face, before the first light,
before the alarm.

Mary Clare Powell

LESBIAN MENOPAUSE

I burrow across our wide bed
and run my hands up your sides,
lift myself onto you, fixing
my breasts to lie amongst yours,
let my weight down slowly, and
kiss the end of your nose.
"I love you," you murmur
and we readjust arms,
always too many for lying together,
too few for making love. And
suddenly all of me that touches
you is wet, water rising
from you, sweet, and I
who was standing on firm ground
just looking around, begin to sink.
I roll off, you sweep the covers back,
lying dew filled and water heavy. Then
you rise out of bed
naked and vertical,
lovely thick water lily

rooted in mud. Porous
stem, weeping leaves,
and extraordinary white
flower on top.

Love Poem: To Violet

Dapple belly sweetheart trout
swimming below my hands,
your daughters swam as fluid
fish inside you once.

Twenty-five years later
your belly, gone to pudding
scarred by love of them,
rises to my long fingers.

The hair which is invisible
with your legs closed
encircles your cunt
like a coral reef.

Wispy sea-smelling grass
through which your little fish swam,
I now approach and open,
my mouth nibbling your stipples.

My white fish, my precious
trout beached on the bed
open gills straining wide,
I will return you to water.

To Be Posted on 21st Street, Between Eye and Pennsylvania

Take this poem down. You can take it and

read it. I wrote it for you passing by, you
standing at the gray plywood construction
wall where it happened. If you'd been here, what
would you have done? Believe me, it was not fun.

And I had been happy, supper at the Trieste
around the corner, that nice Italian place,
cheap cheese ravioli. Was pleasantly hand
in hand with my lover, walking to Eye and 21st,
back to the car. Happy despite hard glances,
angled eyes of two women, next table, unused
to seeing two people together like us. But
we went on, happy. It was a triumph of love.
Holding hands in the street's raw pink glow,
a little like the movies, slow motion angle
on us stepping into the flimsy sidewalk tunnel,
tunnel of love, wedding arch, *arc de triomphe*
after the war, secret passage, honeysuckle
arbor, except it was us in the blunt echo
off the boards, laughing, at walk in the city,
Saturday night.

When some young white men
passed and began to talk at us, derisive.

University, not hard hat, if that's what you
are thinking. Or maybe you're one of them,
reading this now. Why did you try shame?
The mock: *I can't believe it. Can't believe*
it. They're holding hands. Six to us two.
A tongue's scratch scratch, trying to get at
our hearts. Like a movie, sudden threat.
Predictable. I get so tired of this disbelief.
My tongue, faithful in my mouth, said: *Yes, we are.*
The shout: *Lesbians. Lesbians.* Trying to curse
us with our name. Me louder: *That's what we are.*

Around the corner, empty street. Nobody came
with rocks, or dogs. Alone and glad of it,
still holding hands. Around the corner screamed
a car, the men, shouts: *Dykes, dykes.* Have you
ever tried to frighten someone out of their life?
Just having a good time, like shooting at ducks
down by the Bay, or at the office telling jokes.
Nothing personal except to the ones getting hit,
other side of the threat.

                                        But this is a poem
about love, so I should say: In the torn silence
we stood, in the night street, and kissed, solemn,
sweet as any engagement party or anniversary,
stern as the beginning or end of a country's war,
in the risk of who knows who might come and see
us in the open, isolate, tender, exchanging a kiss,
a triumph like no other.

I hope you, here,
have read through, didn't crumple or tear this
up the middle at *lesbian.* I hope you carefully
took this poem down and read it. Now it's a poem
about you, about how there can be a triumph of love.

Liz Queeney

KISSING COCO

It was March. I'd just turned twelve
two weeks before, so I was finally
old enough to think of having
sex with somebody outside
my family. Somebody not male
and not too much older. Somebody
like Coco from Nasella Park.
She was everything I wanted
to be—smart & strong & very tough.
She smoked Lucky Strike non-filters
and could spit as far as any guy.
Already thirteen, so I told her
I was too, pressing my biceps tight
against my sides, trying to make
my breasts appear bigger. Hers were
stretching out her too-tight sweater
(the sweater soft and blue
like her eyes). Catching me staring,

she boldly stared back. She grinned,
and then she winked at me.
I was scared maybe she was
teasing me, scared maybe she wasn't.
My heart swelled up till it almost
hurt. In the past, wanting touch
had only brought pain, but I knew that
I could trust someone who purred
with stray cats. Late at night
on the swingset in Nasella Park,
she opened up two Michelobs,
and asked "Have you ever
gotten drunk?" "Of course! A lot
of times," I lied. I wanted her
to think I was cool. She was
so hot. My mouth was dry.
I sucked down the beer, then
following her lead, I threw the empty
into the bushes. My mouth still dry,
I pulled a Certs from the pocket
of my Levi's, then popped
it into my mouth with relief.
Coco asked, "Ya got any more?" then
seemed all disappointed to hear it was
my last. Without thinking, I offered
her the one in my mouth. "Sure,"
she said as she jumped off the swing.
Instantly her hands were on mine,
the chains of the swing digging into
my palms. I was sweating though

the night air was crisp. My heart beat
so wild I could hardly hear. Coco
commanded, "Give it up," opening
her mouth before mine. The swing
no longer moving, still
everything was swirling
as our lips caressed
and our tongues shared
the Certs & our first kiss.

Shelly Rafferty

Positive (Revisited)

Ignore her when she tells you *no, don't come.*
You know she is just trying to be brave.
The test results will wait for you,
just across the tarmac, just off the plane,
down the long, dark hallway of waiting.
Wear your leather jacket. She used to like that.
Even though, this time, she won't notice.

Go to lunch in an Indian restaurant.
Try to eat.
Hold hands,
even though you haven't been lovers
for too many years to count.
Forget that she's been sleeping with a man,
Forget that she's become a heroin addict,
Forget that once she said, *I don't love you anymore.*

Ask if she is nervous.
  Pick at the dal and chicken Tandoori.
Tell her you'll meet her at the clinic in a couple of hours.
Leave and go get some drinks.
  Drink all afternoon.
  Drive to the clinic alone.
  Sit in the car and smoke.
And cry.
And remember, there is a God.

When she gets there, hold her hand,
Don't say, *this won't change anything.*
In the waiting area, when they come for her,
  wish you could go in with her,
  but obviously, you are not her husband,
  or her wife,
  like you once were.
    Wait.
    Keep waiting.
Suddenly, when she tells you she's ok,
  cry and cry and thank God.
Ask her, *Why didn't you want me to come?*

When she says, because when you went with Paul, he tested positive,
  tell her, *I am not a jinx.*
    Go outside.
    Think about what a glorious October this is.
    Sit in the car beside her, and kiss her,
    With your mouth open, like you used to.

SWEETHEART TOGETHER

Let's crush red roses and sprinkle the petals
On your open bed
Let's open the curtains and let in the last of daylight
Falling west over the Pacific, as I shall always think of it
Slices of orange spice our wine, we touch in disbelief
I'm here beside you.
Dinner, your friends, the strands of your life entwine me
And finally alone, I fold you in my arms, into the night,
Into the here and now of our rose-petal bed.

TOGETHER IN THE WIND

The shore breaks hard beside a dark horizon
The clouds shatter open, the gray pieces grow complex
The wind slushes and everything is still wet

You with your short black hair, in my blue sweater
Your fine Irish features, that blush of English rose

You walk beside me as if you ever had and
I am tempted to fill my cup with wild imaginings
But that's just me isn't it, my verdant green

We walk along the storm so cold yet so alive
September blows crisp and I smile

Happy to be in the wind with you

I Am Loving You

for you, Barbara

I am loving you in the furrowed temperature
of our bodies broadening soft
moving into the trust we fashion
this day and the next.
Holding each other, our children
becoming grandchildren, our grandchildren
growing into this world we want to change,
its broken law of greed and pain.

I am talking about the curve of a breast
in this time when nothing is given
and almost everyone dies before her time.
A trill of sandhill cranes
hold captive breath and sky.
In some ancient cell I know our fingers
moved and touched, remembering.
Perhaps we were sisters, husband and wife,

perhaps we were mother and daughter
father and son, interchangeably.
In a future that requires
successful closure of the Salvadoran war,
all sides in the Middle East
to give something and get something,
I am loving you still
resting against your shoulder's heat.

I am loving you as the sun goes down in Matagalpa,
women like us stroking each other
in old high-ceilinged rooms, jacaranda patios
their walls pocked by the silent caliber
of old battles.
Sun rising over Johannesburg, over Belfast
pale through a narrow ravine on Hopi land
where a child pushes her flock before her
embracing herself against the wind.
Against the winds of change we shape the words
with our mouths that can say these things
because other women said them
and others dreamed them
looking then looking away
holding each other quickly, fear
standing at the door.

Mount Pinatubo's fallout
turns the evening clouds a burning red
above this New Mexico desert
where I am loving you now
long and carefully slow
with words like *wait* and *here* and *yes*
as we tell each other
the world is still a dangerous place.

We will take it one death at a time
claiming only the memory
of our trembling and our rage.

Love Poem

Tell me, bristler, where
do you get such hair
so quick a flare   so strong a tongue

Green eyes   fierce curls
there and here a mole
a girl's
dimples   a warrior's mind

dark blood under gold skin
testing, testing the world
the word

and so to write for you
a pretty sonnet
would be untrue

to your mud-river flashing
over rocks   your delicate
coffee-bushes

and more I cannot know
and some I labor with
and I mean to stay true

even in poems, to you
But there's something more

Beauty, when you were young
we both thought we were young
now that's all done

we're serious now
about death   we talk to her
daily, as to a neighbor

we're learning to be true
with her   she has the keys
to this house   if she must

she can sleep over

Margaret Robison

TWO DAYS BEFORE MY STROKE

for Kendall

Whatever happens, we'll always have this, I said,
wondering at the melodrama of my words.
We stood at the boat rail, eyes filled with ocean.
Neither of us understood the dream that had waked her
nights before my stroke, with a voice that said: *Tell Margaret*
to feel the energy that spirals through you, into her
and back again. This will be only for a little while.
For three months she came to the hospital almost daily.
First as I lay, drugged on morphine, frightened, trapped
in a paralyzed body. Then as I worked to stand,

to speak; to take my first hesitant steps; to begin
to learn to live in a crippled body with a damaged brain.
Only for a little while, the dream voice said.
But still I'm nourished by the memory of Kendall, standing
by my hospital bed in early morning. In her hand,
a bag of ripe strawberries for my breakfast. Rain
streaming down her red rain slicker.

Gold

I woke grieving for my paralyzed leg
with its memories of October walks, grieving
for my paralyzed arm and hand
with their own longings and hopes.
I *will* recover from this stroke,
I tell myself, but fear
lies like lead in my belly
and I look for images
to string together like prayer beads
against despair: wrens
at the feeder, flame
of sumac, evergreens. And making love
in the woods that fall when, for a while,
everything felt possible, the ground thick
with leaves. So gold.
So gold.

I Opened My Hand

I'm startled awake nights
by the touch of my paralyzed hand on my face.
I keep trying to remember how it felt
before it went numb, the feel
of your nipple under my thumb.
Or my fingers, how they would open
with such apparent ease, like the time
you gave me a stone
and I opened my hand, not knowing
that acceptance
would bind me to you forever.

Victoria Alegría Rosales

Your Red, Red Lips

Next time you and I sit down again
to eat Chilean empanadas
and a glass of this red burgundy wine
I'm going to kiss your red, red, burgundy lips
that you paint in front of me.
I'm going to wait until you have painted your red,
red strawberry lips
the color of our menstrual blood
and kiss your lips.

Then I will look at myself in the mirror
And see your large red, burgundy lips stamped on mine
And if you blush, or get angry with me
I won't care for I'll be drunk
with the taste of your red,
red strawberry lips

Cat's Eyes

Ojos de gato
of light brown.
The best dressed
most startling woman in class.
I kept away from you;
I thought you were from my mother's class:
Demanding, uppity, unforgiving of those
different from herself.

Ojos de gato
arched eyebrows
round Inca face
large red mouth
Auracanian blood mixed with white
You came to me.

Ojos de gato
You speak the language of my birth
making me smile at the gentle,
musical rhymes of Gabriela Mistral.
I think of clay idols, chants,

Indian rituals when I am with you.
You said that men have loved you
wanting to give you everything.

But you preferred to be on your own,
Divorced, unmarried and childless.
Fifteen years ago
you left your Andean Mountains
leaving your mother and family behind.
"Why did you reject all that?" I asked.
"To be my own goddess," you replied.

Ojos de gato
Thirty-two years old,
unconcerned about what others might say.
You make me see
that if I were to love a woman again
I should look on the brown earth first.

Muriel Rukeyser

Looking At Each Other

Yes, we were looking at each other
Yes, we knew each other very well
Yes, we had made love with each other many times
Yes, we had heard music together
Yes, we had gone to the sea together
Yes, we had cooked and eaten together

Yes, we had laughed often day and night
Yes, we fought violence and knew violence
Yes, we hated the inner and outer oppression
Yes, that day we were looking at each other
Yes, we saw the sunlight pouring down
Yes, the corner of the table was between us
Yes, bread and flowers were on the table
Yes, our eyes saw each other's eyes
Yes, our mouths saw each other's mouth
Yes, our breasts saw each other's breasts
Yes, our bodies entire saw each other
Yes, it was beginning in each
Yes, it threw waves across our lives
Yes, the pulses were becoming very strong
Yes, the beating became very delicate
Yes, the calling   the arousal
Yes, the arriving   the coming
Yes, there it was for both entire
Yes, we were looking at each other

Kate Rushin

A Pacifist Becomes Militant and Declares War

In the old days
I'd see lovers
Strolling and laughing

I'd watch them and smile
And almost let myself wonder
Why I never felt the way they looked

Now I walk down the street with you
And simply because you are always a woman
I get this teetering feeling

Your sudden
Street corner kiss
Accentuates my hesitation
And I realize that in order to care about you
I have to be everything that is in me

Your laughter underscores the
Sick sinking feeling in my stomach and
I know once and for all
If I walk away
Hide from you
I keep on running from myself

Sometimes
When you kiss me on the street
I feel like a sleepwalker
I feel like I just woke up
And I'm standing on a ledge
Twenty-stories high

And I don't know how in the hell I got here
I say to myself
I say Fool
Why don't you go home and act right
You don't have to be here

Pretend it never happened
Pretend you never felt a thing
Except maybe in a nightmare
Or maybe it was a salty, half-shell dream

Go home and act right
But what for
I can never go back
To what never was
I can't force myself into
Somebody else's image

And If I love you
Even just a little bit
I have to love the woman that I am
I have to reach down deep inside
I have to stand and show myself
I have to walk in the world
There is never any going back
Only going forward into the next day
And the day after that

Your full-length street corner kiss
Is seasoned with excitement
And rebellion

O.K.
Then I'm a rebel
I'm a crazy colored woman
Declaring war on my old ways
On all my fear
My choking
My cringing
My hesitation

I break my fast and admit
That I am hungry
I am hungry to care
To become careless
Careful

So I'm a rebel
Get ready for the insurrection
Get ready for the
Rebellion
Uprising
Riot of my kisses

But Is She Jewish?

My lover practices Yiddish for the sounds,
for the pucker of schmaltz and schmooze
and two fingers over the throat
to test the deepening guttural.
Yes, I say, you're getting close.
That's almost it.
Two women on the fringed settee
and somehow it feels like home.
Boxes upon boxes. My books and
her books, her small breasts.
Marking the days with my hands.

The Last Day of Atonement

I am tired of beating my breast for any supposed
sins against God and against the Cohens, Levys
and Schwartzes of the world, with all their charms
and triangles, pink and black and blue.
There was a time when I'd eat any fruit
that was handed to me. I'd crawl across the desert floor,
a serpent in sheep's clothing, bleating my own ragged need.
From this day forward I'll love the one I love
with all my tongues, my words, my puns,
my grand gestures and unmodulated voice,
the tears, the apples and honey, the sweet

egg bread with yellow raisins, the red sea
of our monthly cycles paced one against the other
in this, our middle age. And brick by brick
we will build our diasporic city. We will pitch
our tents which flap against the wind.

Ruth L. Schwartz

January Vineyards

How our bodies fail to confine our longings,
even in death's season, withholding nothing

How the hills furrow like a cherished body,
leaning into the opened hand of the lake

How the brittle grapevines braid the fields

How the vagina clenches, prayerfully,
around the fingers which have entered it

How the canopy of leaves will bless the fruit,
each grape soft and ready for the mouth

Sex was going to be the landscape
which would make our bodies perfect,
and it has

How savagely I want you, even here,
on the white stretcher, in the pallid hospital

Midnight Supper

Because nothing else can be done,
I peel the tough pale skin from the half-thawed
chicken with my bare hands,
the pink pulp of the meat between my cold
fingers, while the onions and cilantro,
the finely-chopped bell peppers simmer
in coconut milk,
the potato slices soften with gratitude
in their curried sauce.
You said you wished you would die tonight
This was after a long time of not speaking
This was after you said you wished we could make love
the way we used to
It was the first time I saw you openly grieve
the losses your illness has brought between us
after all these months when I raged alone,
so finally, with the immense
mantle of your sadness over both of us,
shaking your body silent, I felt
calmed.
            The sky was darkening; a ring of deep
orange glowed at the horizon,
the crickets were uninterruptible in their symphony
and a slim scythe of a fingernail moon
had appeared, brilliantly,
and I tried to tell you I love you
like I love the world,
all that sunset and moon out there, and the hummingbirds
who come to drink their cherry-colored lives

from the feeder we hung,
and the shooting we hear every night,
the way the shots rise up through the air like furious
knocking on a door which will never be opened,
the sounds of people
killing people out there,
how I take all of it inside me, the whole bitter
shining landscape of our lives together.
I said to you over and over, I love you, until the words
were rain,
and I listened to the crickets, I watched the moon
as it took on more and more of the world's light,
becoming the only beacon of light,
as everything else I could see
leeched out its color into restive sleep,
and then, when you, too, were asleep,
I went down to the kitchen, to the chicken
waiting clammily in its little foam tray, and began
to pull it apart.

The Bed

We build a bed
of plywood and carriage bolts,
hoist ourselves
high above earth, laughing
at the clarity of our dreams.

"Stop at any playground,"
they say, "single out
one little girl at hopscotch
or running down a slide, and think:
you were that young once,
that vulnerable."

We admire our bed,
its four corners fit together
in peace, the strength
of its wide platform. We inhale
the perfume of fresh-cut wood, dive
naked into grandma's quilt.

"Forgive yourself
your lack of vigilance in the night,
flesh that violated yours.
See how small you were,
how your white socks
dribbled into red shoes."

Nothing breaks when we love.
We fling ourselves
into mornings as if crazed,
confront the tired faces of night.
In our new bed,
we are miraculous.

A Poverty of Robins

A robin appeared in Harlem the same day
you slaughtered the only lightning bug
on the block—instinctively, the way
grown men destroy whole villages out of
fear. Now I watch you flail in the backyard
to avoid a diving bee, imagine
the sting of a childhood without yards
full of bumblebees to play in. When
that red breast landed on that patch of grass,
hopping the way robins do, searching
for an early breakfast worm, you said:
"What the hell is that?" We'd just been well
fed ourselves on buckwheat and molasses.
For a moment, I thought you must be kidding.

For a moment, I thought you must be kidding
over pizza bianca in the village, flanked
by your laughing friends—musicians making
jazz for women-loving women. You drank
Pepsi to my ankles in French,
Italian, Spanish. I thought you were
a genius, pushy. I'd loved you since
St. Mark's Place, since you showed up sober
and looking for a job, a miracle
and sexy in studs and slicked-back hair. I'd
wanted you, and there you were on Macdougal,
yelling flagrant compliments at my
body in three different languages.
If you'd been male, I'd have despised your guts.

If you'd been male, I'd have despised your guts,
and we'd be slightly less visible—
therefore, safer in Manhattan. But
who knows? It seems Black and white couples
attract attention everywhere—at least
when they step gingerly out of shadows.
Once, we were waiting on 119th
for a gypsy cab and crazy Cornelius
Crowley came tottering off the curb
with pointed finger to lecture you
on the sins of sleeping with a white woman.
You became famous that night in Harlem
for your fleetness of foot and biting words,
the blade that emerged like a friend beside you.

The blade that emerged like a friend beside you
lay buried beneath our clothes the day
we first made love. The sky was rare blue,
the air bright as country air. I gave
you violets and tiger lilies, jewelry
of amethyst and moonstone, cowrie shell
and abalone pearl. You gave me
lapis and sunflowers, tiny bells
of polished gold. Our bed was sanctuary
from the ridicule around us, the hate
as daily as sunrise. We opened
to the lawlessness and luxuries
of love, the delightful possibilities and
a robin appeared in Harlem the same day.

THESE FADED BLUE

flowers
on the sheet
this Sunday

morning light
this house
still as though

you were off
in the shower or
had run out

for breakfast
milk
my hand

smooths
the wrinkles
as I make

the bed
with such easy
motion

would I
bring you
back

Elizabeth Responds to the Separation

Your absence stirs up frequent conversation
in my brain. I talk to you in rhyme.
I state the facts. I ask for explanation,

my imaginary friend. Silence is aggravation:
winter *sans* snow, the mountain far too steep to climb.
Your absence leads to curious conversation

we would never have at home. Revelation
sprouts in unexpected spots, its bloom sublime.
I state more facts. Your explanation

slips a crocus in my hand. My admiration
escalates. I talk to you (why do they stare?) in mime.
Your absence turns me into conversation

with a cow, a fence. I make a declaration
to the moon at dawn. O love! Time
takes her time, that's fact. No explanation

comes for why I miss you so. Infatuation
ages through the years, like wine.
Your absence puts an end to conversation.
I am the fact. You are the explanation.

Longing

I am missing you, tonight
The room is void of your
moans and laughter
I am missing you, tonight
Need your thick, brown hair
to wrap round my fingers
Need your dark smile
to break forth all over me
Need those thick, strong thighs
to hold me up to the sky
Need your breasts rubbed
round my face
Need your calling out my name
Need your back arched under me
like a strong, black bridge
linking our African pasts.
I am missing you tonight.
Please come to me.

Sides

Sometimes, I require nothing more
than
to have you near me,
making love gently

lightly touching, tracing lines
around your heart
and breasts;
feeling your tender
fragrant, steady breathing;
moistening my fingers
with your anticipation
of things to come.

Sometimes, I require nothing less
than
all of you
taking me inside
pushing past all walls,
making furious and passionate
rhythms
hearing you breathe heavy
and unsteady
in my ear;
tensions exploding
as you wet my face
with your trust.

Linda Smukler

Mom's Best Friend

It's as if you went up into your neighbor's house when you were 15 years old and she was 10 years older and had 2 children and yet she looked at you and said I know you   maybe you were the baby-sitter or maybe you were just your mother's daughter and maybe you had already cut your hair and maybe just maybe she was the woman next door who was your mom's best friend whose eyes really did look into yours   who brushed by and was very official about the touch because at first she was completely capable of passing you by   but maybe you were a little bit bold and maybe she showed you the long narrow hall to the linen closet to the basement to the laundry room and stopped as she looked down into the washing machine when suddenly she turned and you stared at her wanting and you did not say anything and then she looked down again and said into the washing machine   You know I don't   and could not say anything else   you reached out and touched her hand and she drew you close and kissed you   she said I know your mom and you said I know you know my mom   she kissed you again and her son ran down the stairs   she pushed you away and started pulling laundry out of the washing machine   her son said Mom where's my tennis racket?   she answered I don't know   Look in the kitchen closet   she said her words so calmly that the kid went upstairs to look again while her sun-dark hand barely touched yours resting on the white enamel where you both waited as if your entire lives depended on the discovery of a tennis racket lost deep inside a kitchen closet

EARTHQUAKE WEATHER

on my way over to yr house
dry leaves sleep
silent on the burning sidewalk
until i kick them awake

through the hot smog sometimes
there is a quiet smell
like wet clean laundry
being hung out to dry

on a day like this
when new shoes hurt
from the heat
& hair sticks damp
on the back of my neck
your tongue tastes
so cool

like the white fuzzy part of strawberries
or the slip on an avocado pit, you are
under the moons of my fingernails & deep
down in my lungs, i feel you like pollen
or blue veins. for you i will jump & stay
up there like a hollywood special effect
but here now in the stratosphere i am
frightened, your planets and milky ways
so alien violet & perfect. i will not come
down, but cry scratching at your starry
kitchen table until i have written a love
song for you, one unpublic & not like those
outside split-end top 40, a song that tastes
like your very inside.

June Blue Spruce

PREGNANT SEX

I want to spend eight days tracing
the lines of your face,
following the map of blue veins
on your swollen breasts.
your nipples push
into my mouth.   you urge me
to suck the milk down.

your belly heaps up,
hardens to rock with your shaking
orgasm.   you cry
like you never used to—
coming was once quick with you,
earthquake
and aftershocks.
now you are big and slow,
and you have to ask the baby,
wait for the tiny feet
to flutter inside you
before you can
come a second time.
you watch me,
heaving hot beside you, and smile.
I was once
the slow one, the one who said no.
you fill up, day by day, growing
open, preparing
for the coming, the letting go, the gush
of baby and blood.

we take time tracing
the lines of your skin
stretched taut,
tuned fine.
we learn from this little one
new music.

The Erotics of Morning

The wild world pours, it curls, it pearls
an outburst of wetness in a woman's crotch
the crotch of the thought at the crotch of the tree
where the tree bends and arcs in a frank hang
one bendable trunk across the world's one stream.

The thought is elastic, contractable, sure
to quiver like water at anyone's touch
I quiver like water, I hiss like ice
cubes shot through with slivers of air
under pressure, under the pulse
of a hammer, a blender, a late startled love.

Traffic noise, ear pain, some sort of horn,
winter forever in a screen window dawn.

Home Tongue

When I kiss her,
she pushes a story into my mouth.

I mean to
elaborate.

CRADLESONG

You cradle me in your arms and I tell you
I am afraid of a hysterectomy
how I know it's safe & 30% of the women
have these fibroids but still
it's scary
like walking home in the late night dark
down Broadway from a movie: no trees
stirring
shadows moving
imaginary six foot men leaping out behind
grabbing me
no longer will I be whole.

You cradle me in your arms and say you'll love me
even when
my hair turns gray, my breasts are sagging
we'll grow old together
not to worry
you never loved me for my beauty
you distrusted blonde-haired, blue-eyed
goys.

You cradle me in your arms and I cry
I fear I'll be considered sexless
despised, rejected, repressed, ignored,
like the crones, the witches, the Hecates
in our culture.

Now I cradle you in my arms and begin
ever more
to love you
for what is happening here between us
is more than any hysterectomy could take
from me.

May Swenson

Mornings Innocent

I wear your smile upon my lips
arising on morning's innocent
Your laughter overflows my throat
Your skin is a fleece about me
With your princely walk I salute the sun
People say I am handsome

Arising on mornings innocent
birds make the sound of kisses
Leaves flicker light and dark like eyes

I melt beneath the magnet of your gaze
Your husky breath insinuates my ear
Alert and fresh as grass I wake

and rise on mornings innocent
The strands of the wrestler
run golden through my limbs
I cleave the air with insolent ease
With your princely walk I salute the sun
People say I am handsome

Four-Word Lines

Your eyes are just
like bees, and I
feel like a flower.
Their brown power makes
a breeze go over
my skin. When your
lashes ride down and
rise like brown bees'
legs, your pronged gaze
makes my eyes gauze.
I wish we were
in some shade and
no swarm of other
eyes to know that
I'm a flower breathing
bare, laid open to
your bees' warm stare.
I'd let you wade
in me and seize
with your eager brown
bees' power a sweet
glistening at my core.

CONFESSIONS OF AN ESCAPE ARTIST

Loving you is a matter
of muscle and marrow
tendon and bone
of cells dividing
in the dark hallways
of self

You could tell me to leave.
I would pull down my brown
canvas bag
throw in the model galleon
my father made
sitting on the back stoop
of a falling down house
in west Texas
throw in my IRS returns
for the last seven years
my socks
my fortune cookie
my Old English Sheep Dog
my Visa card
with the receding limit

I could do all this.
I could throw this bag in the back
of my truck
gun my engine
till it sobbed
release the emergency
back out
in a blue cloud
drive to west Texas
and still I would not
be gone

Kitty Tsui

GLORIOUSLY

first day of the new year.
we are guests for the night.
bedding together,
down bags on tatami
in a meditation room
warmed by a blazing woodstove.

moonlight through
rice paper shutters
falls on our bodies
as we talk and touch
and taste each other
for the first time.

mouth on mouth, thigh
on thigh, hand on breast,
my fingers circling
your nipple, a long moan.
I take you in my mouth,
a sharp inhale of breath.

shoulder to thigh
I push my tongue
inside your depths,
hands on your ass,
fingers down your crack
and feel your passion rise.

I sink my teeth
into bicep muscle,
feel your wetness,
stroke your lips,
tongue soft folds, then
part and penetrate you.

tongue inside mouth,
hand on breast,
fingers circling clitoris.
how do you like to come? i ask.
you reply simply:
gloriously.

DRAGON LOVER

you are
solid bicep
round ass
untiring arm
insatiable hunger
raw energy
exquisite pleasure
fluid power
rock hard
pulsating inside me.

you are
soft lips
unyielding tongue
knowing tickle
gentle touch
rough play
exquisite pleasure
fluid power
rock hard
pulsating inside me.

you are
brown skin
long legs
hard thighs
demanding fingers
delicious fist
exquisite pleasure

fluid power
rock hard
pulsating inside me.

you are
tough sister
rough fantasy
rowdy lover
best friend
riding partner
exquisite pleasure
fluid power
rock hard
pulsating inside me

THE BATH

Only the sound of you
splashing while I shift
from foot to foot in the cold
kitchen where the windows
have frosted so I can't see out.
I pull the string overhead and light
floods the cold, hard surfaces
each time, too bright.
You are taking one of your famous
baths, as you do
when you are tired or cold
or uneasy in the night. Newly washed,
your red hair, your red hair
sings to me
through the closed door and the steam
which seeps out
under it.
I know it is late but your hair

is not tired. And though I am very
cold, I am happy
being sung to.
Soon, but not yet,
I will walk into the bathroom,
sit down on the blue toilet seat
and ask you something.
You in the tub,
naked and wet, your skin
shining and freckled,
your eyes closed, your glasses far away
in another room, your singing hair
swept back by water,
converging where your nape
curves into the tub's curve, a thin washcloth
spread over your chest.

Pencil and Blue Crayon

Let the last drawing I make with pencil and blue crayon
be of you in the bath.

Let the weather be fine in February and August.

Let all of us belong to the sunlit now and move
from surprise to surprise.

Let the yellow dining rooms where we drink wine
have red tablecloths and balconies.

Let all I cannot say open me in your arms.

Let me sit in an old beachchair touching the green present.

Sarah Van Arsdale

Lullabye

Each nightfall brings a little loss, lifting
you relentlessly from the perisphere
of you, here: your blue-checked sheets, sere
pages of a book, seed cake and the shifting
street lamp's shadow grid as lit through stiff
glass, tangle of your brain cells clearing
paths continually for nuances of thought. You fear
the loss awaiting you in sleep's deep heft.

As you shift beneath the sheet, remember this: stars
will breathe hard down your window panes all night,
while you sail dreamward to a sky the deep
blue the girl in you recalls, and the scarred
moon's face shelters us all. Soon you'll reunite
with book and cake and sheet. Tomorrow will keep.
Hush now big girl, go to sleep.

Diane Vance

Favorite Words

The letter you sent said tell me your favorite words.
I tell you words fail again and again but I would try
and say, honest, come to me honest, I couldn't stand less.
Or mouth, I will pass them from my mouth to yours sweet
and warm. Come closer, take the word mouth against your
skin and mouth to me your favorite words like earth
that's damp and smells like earth where I would lie
with you my hands in it, the way my life is in it
earth me closer down in dirt where my life holds me
to it, smell sweet earth, I want it wet against my
skin. Could I tell you more than this,
is there everything you'd like to know? I would choose
the sounds to please you, try to say what it would mean
to believe you want to know my favorite words.

Tell me more I hear you say, more, I answer yes,
yes, but listen, the clouds are low or listen, the sky
is dark tonight, the stars are out. Like the night I
came to you then left because I felt no comfort except
to walk out and out again into the night's low clouds,
spring flowers full in bloom against the dark they move
me and I miss you in it. My hands are awkward, resist
knowing your skin, at first afraid they had forgotten the
way to touch sweet sweat against another skin, as if they
would protect me in my fear. Listen, I walk quiet through
the night, think one thousand words, a vocabulary of grief
and loss still it brought me back to you, my will to trust
I could try again with one who would ask to hear my words
against the lies and pain, the hurt, intended or not
outside this place where we have found each other sweetly
mouthing words in the time that's in-between.

Chocolate Waters

First Woman

First woman
Your name was not Eve
You did not offer me
apples
You touched me
I quivered
Then suffered
Then regretfully

threw up
I denied you
more than
three times
You confessed
to your priest
who laughed
You confessed
your love
to me
I did not
laugh
when you threw me
out of
your life
like an apple
I wrote you
a love song
with a man's name
instead of yours
First woman
Your name
was Sharon
I sprang
half-grown
from the
touch
of your
first woman's
hands

Separation

You're
asleep across town
Light switched off
Book in lap
Coffee gone
Cat at your feet
Arm around pillow
Job tomorrow.
I'm
awake across town
Light switched off
Book in lap
Coffee turned to Scotch
Cat at my feet
Arm around pillow
Job tomorrow.

Backs of my fingers
through your
curly hair.

AMISH COUNTRY

Although we have never touched my body knows yours.
Our eyes meet too often for too long in the gray hallways
Asking the only question you cannot answer.
Eyes always know eyes first.

You lean toward the copier,
Never cursing it as all the others do.
Working here has enlarged your vocabulary
Beyond what the Plain People,
Your half-escaped ancestry,
Would admit to their straitened list.
You know the words, though you can't remember them.

Your plain plaid dress stretches neatly
Into a small treat for my two eyes,
A gift you pretend you are not giving me.
Watching you has enlarged my vocabulary
Which has too many words for "maybe."

Someday you'll quit this job
For one with no clients and no cursers,
And throw a farewell dinner for yourself.

At the party I will look at you full
Measuring my plain brown eyes against
Your changing blue gray green
While I offer to help you clean up
After everyone else is gone.

Over the steaming dishwater
You'll tell me about the heavy meals
The many courses, the sweet and sour relishes
You were raised on. I'll ask you why you left.
You won't tell me. Instead, you'll walk toward me
Raising your eyes to mine, dropping your towel.

And then I will place my worldly hand
On the site of your thoughts
And your unwoken curses
My worldly lips on your red and yellow throat
Prepared at last to taste and to number
Your seven sweets and your seven sours.

Aryn A. Whitewolf

BUS STOP LOVER

It happened in a heartbeat
years of passion rolled into a speck of time
our eyes met/ we knew desire
made love/ threw parties/ made friends/ rode horses
walked on a hundred beaches
ate cheesecake in bed/ bathed each other in champagne
raised a family/ changed flat tires
adopted a puppy/ grew our own vegetables/ shopped for
curtains/ gave each other flowers
played softball/ cards/ monopoly/ backgammon/ went to
drive-ins/ talked baby talk/ kissed

cried when the bird died/ wrapped presents/ argued sometimes
        threw snowballs/ sailed/ had pillow fights
told each other I LOVE YOU every day/ lived and loved
        openly as lesbians for over forty years
all in the blink of an eye/ all in an instant/ a heartbeat
        then your bus came/ and you were gone

Brooke Wiese

Jazzed Up

Baby, seeing you
rounding the corner
at Broadway and Astor Place
in your business suit and briefcase,
you come towards me
in spike-heeled pumps
   click   click   click
your stocking seams straight as a Catholic.
Oh, you state-of-the-art corporate dyke!
Seeing you,
I ain't feelin' no blues tonight.

Ten feet away from me you stop
and lean against the lamppost
like in a B movie.
Apparently engrossed with the hem of your skirt
and with seeming disregard for me
you hike the skirt higher

flashing just enough thigh
to make my nipples hard
and the hairs stand up on the back of my neck.
My heart skips a beat and goes
   thunk   thunk   thunk
and I weave towards you
like a Bowery drunk
tripping over sidewalk cracks
or my own two feet, while you,
trying not to laugh,
bend to smooth a pleat.

I know this poem is not
politically correct
but baby, I don't care.
On the corner where
Astor and Broadway intersect
all the people stop and stare
at you—this is nothing new:
a group of college kids
with their bottom lips on their chins,
East Village hard core punks
with spiked and orange hair and pins
stuck in places I wouldn't dare,
a queen with one hand on her hip
and one in the air,
whose silver bracelets
   chink   chink   chink
as she passes by, a study in pink,
and winks at you—
and even the lady in blue,
yes, the beat cop too.

All of them looking
looking at you.

Oh, they know you're pretty
but I know it's me
you've come to meet
and when you kiss me there in the street
it is sweeter than sweet.
And they just stare harder,
hardly discrete.
Even the lady cop.
Well let them stare till they drop
'cause I swear
kissing you
I get so
jazzed
up.

Suddenly! Your Hand

In the clear, near-dawn August air
a Checker cab slows and drops his fare
who stumbles off, unaware

of our luck, this early hour, to catch his ride.
Sir, take us please to the other side
of the river that flows so black and wide,

we say. The cabbie shrugs and yawns.
He checks his watch, taps it. Resigned, he longs
for a signed promise of sleep at dawn's

coming. He flips the flag and makes
the turn at Fifty-seventh Street—he takes
the upper road, and humming, never breaks.

This old bridge has carried graver load.
The cab's wheels whir on the ribbed, steel road—
the tires sing softly in tickety-tick code

the praises of this eight-crowned span.
Over my shoulder, westward, an
avalanche of mid-town lights is only where we've been.

Nestled in the wide back seat
we head for Queens, where lovers fight and love in Greek
and trains careen above the silent streets.

Unannounced, unmistakable, unplanned—
Suddenly! your hand
on mine and I lose my sense of self-command

till I take a breath and count to ten
and remember the city lights at my back, and say amen,
as I hear the tickety-tick of tires again.

Julia Willis

SWEET(S)

HER/SHE
KISSES.

LOADED DICE

Sugar,
you have more
games
than Nintendo
ever dreamed of.
Just when I think
I've got the
old one mastered,
damned
if there isn't
a new one
ready and waiting.
So,
being a
sporting woman,
I ante up.
It's
your game
and you get to
define the rules
we play by.
One
wrong move
and I get
jumped.
But then,
it is your game,
isn't it?

Here in the Forest

Lie down with me
on a blanket
of long needled pine.
Let me cover you
with multi-colored leaves.
The moon and stars
will dim their light
to shield us.
Here in the darkness
skin color
goes unnoticed.
Here in the forest
my Indian ways
are natural.

Terry Wolverton

Black Slip

She told me she had always fantasized
about a woman in a black slip.
It had to do with Elizabeth Taylor
in *Butterfield Eight.*

She came to my house with a huge box
gift-wrapped with gigantic ribbons.
Inside, a black slip.

Slinky, with lace across the bodice.
She told me how she was embarrassed
in the department store,
a woman in men's pants
buying a black slip clearly not intended for herself,
and about the gay men in line behind her,
sharing the joke.

She asked me to try it on.
I took it into the bathroom, slipped it over my head.
I stared at myself for a long time
before I came out of the bathroom
walked over to her
lying on the bed.

That was the first time. It got easier.
The black slip was joined by a blue slip
then a red one
then a long lavender negligee, the back slit to there.

I wore them to bed.
In the morning she would smile and say
how much she loved waking up next to a woman in a slip.
The black slip remained our favorite.
We always made love when I wore the black slip.

Once I showed up at her door late at night
wearing a long coat
with only the black slip underneath.

One night I cooked dinner at her apartment
wearing nothing but the black slip
and red suede high heels.

It was always the first thing to pack when we went on
vacation.

And she used to make me promise
that if we ever broke up
I'd never wear that slip for anyone else.

I don't know where it is now.

Stripped of that private skin
when we broke up
I never went back to claim it.

I think she must have
packed it
given it
thrown it
away.

On bad days I imagine her
sliding it over the head of some new love
whispering about Elizabeth Taylor
and waking up to a woman in a slip.

Or perhaps
it's still there
draped on the back of the door.

A sinuous shadow.

A moan in the dark.

Merle Woo

UNTITLED

In the deepest night and a full moon,
at once riding the flying mare and being her
my own pumping broad wings, ascending higher—

My legs around that great horse's neck
not riding
but my body singing down under
in front of the beautiful dark head
feeling her moist tongue in my center—

I am risking my life for these moments,
my head possibly dashed against the rocks.

Now riding with our rhythms matching,
the exertion of her back's muscles and
the mounting pulsations between my thighs—

Higher and soaring through mist and above mountains
shaped like jagged spires
the cold thin air ripping through my lungs—

We finish
And you lay your head on my thigh,
your wings enfolding my legs, and we rest.

DC

On your knees
On my back
Between your thighs
Between my eyes
Lips on lips
I venture inside.
Tongue to twitch
Linger and ride
Bitter showers
Slide down the sides
Tingling,
tracing
Adrenalines rise.
Down my front
Up your spine
Navels aligned
If not the minds
Nape,
lobe
Hands entwined
Toes touching
Bodies combined
Beads of shivers
Tantalize
Squeeze and tighten
Analyze

Flesh in flesh
Breath on sigh
Equal bodies
Superior signs
Both top and bottom
Electrified.

Shay Youngblood

TWO TONGUES

and this is what she said . . .

Kiss my smile in the morning before day flies through the
window.
In the evening spread your perfume upon my thighs.
Open all your shuttered windows in the dark and silent night.
Light my way with a flame that never dies. Never dies.
Never dies.

at the same time she said this . . .

Besa mi sonrisa por la mañana, antes de que el día vuele por
la ventana.
En la tarde, unta tu perfume a lo largo de mis piernas.
Abre tus cristales empañados en la noche silenciosa y oscura.
Alumbra mi sendero con una llama que nunca muere.
Nunca muere. Muere nunca.

and that is when the bed burst into flames.

Promises, Promises

This is not a love poem.
This is a fever on the page
my heart is made of blue glass
filled with love, such a tender thing,
so sweet and furious
so hard and unforgiving.

This is not a love poem.
This is each one of my fingers exercising inside of you,
unfolding in your womb like a flower,
palm opening for more of you.

Open the book
turn the page and leave your mark in wild, dark
and tangled places,
between my legs, my lips, five hands down my back.
Hide yourself inside me,
wake me up.
Let the neighbors know you love me,
breathe high C arias into my throat,
let me come with you.

Turn your back on me and imagine
the things I will do to you
from behind,
in the kitchen,
against the wall,
in the upstairs closet,
on the floor,

in the bathtub,
underwater,
with reverence and grace,
patience and mercy.

I am yours and this promise is for you.

Yvonne Zipter

Green Couch

It will be on the green couch.
I will be sitting, legs folded
like hands on a lap, waiting,
leaning toward your voice,
a vivid goat reaching for green leaves.
The lamp will go out, surprising us,
as if a sudden gust had quieted a candle.
We will take it as a sign.
I will hold your face,
my thumbs fitting easily
into the hollows of your cheek,
fingers decorating your neck
like piano keys begging to be played.
The couch, like a cupped hand,
will hold us, found snails, spiraling,
spiraled, the street light
glancing off protective shells.

When we think of this later,
we will remember our first kiss
in a wash of green, we
twin pearls
in the fleshy jaws of an oyster, no trace
of sand remaining.

The Cupola

I want to make love to you in the cupola,
in this bare room, so small
we can fill it easily,
no corner untouched, with our passion.
Bare, as your skin, cream-colored walls
marked from all that came before
and flat, wide boards holding us firmly below,
honest in their matter-of-fact brown and dusty faces.
I want to make love to you in this bare room
hiding nothing.

I want to make love to you beneath these twelve windows,
bold in their excess, the sun
adding lines and angles
to your breast as it answers
the cup of my hand. The sharp
turns of collarbone and elbow
carving their image on my eye:

I want to see it all: the harsh light
of noon underscoring every scar;
the reflective light
at dusk, touching you softly
echoing my hand; the selfish light
of moon, tracing you on the floor
until I can see where you've been.

I want to make love to you in the cupola,
windows open, your sighs and moans resonating
on the stones of the courtyard below,
filling my ears, the room, the air,
boards beneath us
creaking out loud, telling our secret
and we won't care.

Donna Allegra has had her writing published in the anthologies *Home Girls: A Black Feminist Anthology*; *Sportsdykes*; *Out of the Class Closet: Lesbians Speak*; *Lavender Mansions: Forty Contemporary Gay and Lesbian Short Stories*; *Fat Women Speak*; and *All the Ways Home: Short Stories about Children and the Lesbian and Gay Community.*

Paula Gunn Allen is the author of the poetry collections *Shadow Country* and *Skin and Bones*; and the nonfiction books *Grandmothers of the Light: A Medicine Woman's Sourcebook* and *The Sacred Hoop: Recovering the Feminine in American Indian Traditions.* She is also the editor of *Spider Woman's Granddaughters: Traditional Tales and Contemporary Writing by Native American Women.*

Dorothy Allison is the author of the novel *Bastard Out of Carolina* (1992 National Book Award Finalist in Fiction), the book of essays *Skin* (Lambda Literary Award), the short story collection *Trash* (double Lambda Literary Award), and the collection of poetry *The Women Who Hate Me: Poetry 1980–1990.*

Paula Amann has had her poetry published in the anthologies *Sister/Stranger: Lesbians Loving Across the Lines*; *Jane's Stories: An Anthology of Work by Midwestern Women*; and *Sisters*.

Ghazala Anwar received an M.A. in English Literature from Aligarh Muslim University in India. "songs towards you" is her first published poem.

V.K. Aruna has had her writing published in the anthologies *The Very Inside: An Anthology of Writing by Asian and Pacific Islander Lesbian and Bisexual Women*; *Our Feet Walk the Sky*; *Pearls of Passion*; and *The Third Wave: Feminist Perspectives on Racism*.

Jane Barnes is the author of *Extremes*, a poetry collection. She is the recipient of a PEN Syndicated Fiction Award, and teaches at the Boston Center for Adult Education.

Judith Barrington is the author of two poetry collections: *Trying to Be an Honest Woman* and *History and Geography*, and the editor of the anthology *An Intimate Wilderness: Lesbian Writers on Sexuality*. She is the director of "The Flight of the Mind," summer writing workshops for women.

Ellen Bass is the author of *Our Stunning Harvest* (poetry) and *The Courage to Heal: A Guide for Women Survivors of Child Sexual Abuse* (nonfiction) and the coeditor of *No More Masks! An Anthology of Poems by Women*. Her literary awards include the 1980 Elliston Book Award for Poetry from the University of Cincinnati.

Robin Becker is the author of two poetry collections: *Giacometti's Dog* and *Backtalk*. She has received fellowships from the National Endowment for the Arts and the Massachusetts Artists Foundation. She is the poetry editor of *The Women's Review of Books* and an Associate Professor of English at Pennsylvania State University.

Sally Bellerose is the author of a chapbook of poetry, *Sex Crimes*. Her writing has been published in the anthologies *The Poetry of Sex*; *The Persistent Desire: A Femme-Butch Reader*; *Women on Women 2*; and in the journals *Common Lives/Lesbian Lives*, *Hurricane Alice*, and *Sinister Wisdom*. In 1995 she received a Fellowship in Creative Writing from the National Endowment for the Arts.

Becky Birtha is the author of *The Forbidden Poems*, as well as two collections of fiction, *Lovers' Choice* and *For Nights Like This One*. Her writing has appeared in the anthologies *Breaking Ice: An Anthology of Contemporary African American Fiction*; *Women on Women*; *The Single Mother's Companion*; and *Home Girls: A Black Feminist Anthology*. Her literary awards include fellowships from the National Endowment for the Arts and the Pennsylvania Council on the Arts.

Margaret Cardea Black received an M.F.A. in Creative Writing from the University of Iowa Writer's Program. Her poetry has been published in the anthologies *Wanting Women: An Anthology of Erotic Lesbian Poetry* and *The Poetry of Sex*, and in the journals *The Kenyon Review*, *The Beloit Poetry Journal*, *The Southern Poetry Review*, *Sinister Wisdom*, and *Fireweed*.

Nancy Boutilier is the author of a poetry collection, *According to Her Contours*, which was a Lambda Literary Award

Finalist. She attended Harvard/Radcliffe College and the Bread Loaf School of English. Her writing has appeared in the journals *Bay Area Reporter*, *Sphere*, and *Deneuve*.

Olga Broumas is the author of *Beginning with O* (Yale Younger Poets Award), *Soie Sauvage*, *Pastoral Jazz*, *Perpetua* and *Sappho's Gymnasium*. She is the recipient of fellowships from the National Endowment for the Arts and the Guggenheim Foundation.

Jayne Relaford Brown received an M.F.A. in Creative Writing from San Diego State University. Her poetry has appeared in the anthologies *I Am Becoming the Woman I've Wanted*; *The Poetry of Sex*; *Wanting Woman: An Anthology of Erotic Lesbian Poetry*; and *El Vuelo del Aguila/The Flight of the Eagle* and in the journals *The Minnesota Review*, *Pacific Review*, and *Hurricane Alice*.

Melissa Cannon has had poems published in the anthologies *A Formal Feeling Comes* and *Sleeping with Dionysus*.

Lori Cardona has had writing published in the journals *esto no tiene nombre*, *Conmocion*, *The L Connection*, and *Speaking Heart to Heart*.

Ana Marie Castañon has had writing published in the journals *Sinister Wisdom* and *The Evergreen Chronicles*.

Laura Castellanos del Valle is a Civil Rights attorney. "Last Kiss" and "Missing You" are her first published poems.

Chrystos is the author of the collections of poetry *Not Vanishing*, *Dream On*, *In Her I Am*, *Fugitive Colors*, and *Fire*

Power. Her writing has been published in the anthology *A Gathering of Spirit: A Collection by North American Indian Women*. Her literary awards include a National Endowment for the Arts Fellowship, a Barbara Deming Memorial Grant, a Lannan Foundation Grant for Poetry, and the Audre Lorde International Poetry Competition Award.

Elizabeth Clare received her M.F.A. in Creative Writing from Goddard College. Her poems and essays have been published in the journals *Hanging Loose*, *The Disability Rag*, *Sojourner*, *Sinister Wisdom*, *The Evergreen Chronicles*, and in the anthology *Sister/Stranger: Lesbians Loving Across the Lines*.

Cheryl Clarke is the author of four poetry collections: *Narratives: Poems in the Tradition of Black Women*, *Humid Pitch*, *Living as a Lesbian*, and *Experimental Love*, which was a Lambda Literary Award Finalist.

Martha Courtot received an M.A. in English Literature from Sonoma State University. Her writing has appeared in the anthologies *Lesbian Poetry* and *New Lesbian Writing* and in the journals *The American Voice*, *Heresies*, and *Sinister Wisdom.*

Patricia Donegan is the author of two poetry collections: *Without Warning* and *Bone Poems (Mini-Cantos)*. She received a Fulbright Scholarship to cotranslate and write a book, *Chiyo-ni Woman Haiku Master*, on Japan's greatest woman haiku poet.

Amy Edgington has had her writing published in the anthologies *Wanting Women: An Anthology of Erotic Lesbian*

Poetry; *Range of Motion: An Anthology of Disability Poetry*; *Prose and Art*; and *Women and Death: 108 American Poets*, and in the journals *Common Lives/Lesbian Lives*, *Sinister Wisdom*, and *Heresies*.

Ana Bantigue Fajardo has had her writing published in the journals *Big Red Rag*, *Twanas*, and *The Phillipine News*, and in the anthology *The Very Inside: An Anthology of Writing by Asian and Pacific Islander Lesbians and Bisexual Women*.

Lori Faulkner is the author of a collection of poetry, *We Talked About Being a Woman*. Her poetry has also been published in the journal *Common Lives/Lesbian Lives*.

Folisade is the author of *Gifts from Spirit* and *Quicksand! African American Lesbian Erotica*. Her literary awards include the Black Rennaisance Poet Award given by the International Black Writers and Artists Inc. of San Francisco and the Black Writers' Award given by the Peninsula Book Club.

Beatrix Gates is the author of *native tongue* and *Shooting at Night*. Her writing has appeared in the anthology *Gay and Lesbian Poetry in Our Time* and in the journals *The Kenyon Review* and *The Nation*.

Shahara Lauren Godfrey has had her poetry published in the literary magazine *Catalyst*.

Lynn Goldfarb received a Master of Arts in Liberal Studies from Wesleyan University. "Poem With an Attitude" is her first published poem.

Jewelle Gomez is the author of a novel, *The Gilda Stories*, (double Lambda Literary Award); a collection of essays, *Forty-three Septembers*, and *Oral Traditions: Poems Selected and New*.

Melinda Goodman is the author of a collection of poetry entitled *Middle Sister* and the recipient of an Astraea Emerging Lesbian Writers Fund Award for Poetry. Her poetry has been published in the anthologies *The Femme Mystique* and *Gay and Lesbian Poetry in Our Time*. She teaches Literacy and Creative Writing at Hunter College in New York City.

Adele Gorelick writes a column entitled "What We Are Reading" for *Woman's Monthly*, a Washington/Baltimore periodical.

Janice Gould is the author of a collection of poetry entitled *Beneath My Heart*. Her writing has been published in the anthology *A Gathering of Spirit: A Collection by North American Indian Women*. Her literary awards include a National Endowment for the Arts Fellowship and the Astraea Emerging Lesbian Writers Fund Award for Poetry.

Tzivia Gover studied Creative Writing at Columbia University. Her writing has been published in the anthology *The Femme Mystique* and in the journals *The Evergreen Chronicles* and *Peregrine*.

Judy Grahn is the author of *The Work of a Common Woman*; *The Queen of Wands*; *The Queen of Swords*; *Mundane's World*; *The Highest Apple: Sappho and the Lesbian Poetic Tradition*; *Another Mother Tongue: Gay Words, Gay Worlds*; and *Blood, Bread and Roses: How Menstruation Created the World.* Her literary awards include a National Endowment for the Arts Fellowship, American Poetry Review Poem of the Year Award, Lambda Literary Award, and American Library Association Gay Book of the Year Award.

Pamela Gray is the author of a poetry chapbook, *the lesbian breakup manual*, and the author of the screenplay for *Stone Butch Blues*. Her writing has been published in the anthologies *Love's Shadow*, *The Femme Mystique*, and *Naming the Waves* and in the journal *Sinister Wisdom*. Her literary awards include the 1993 Women in the Moon Poetry Prize, a 1994 Drama-Logue Critics Award for Playwriting, and the First Place 1992 Samuel Goldwyn Screenwriting Award.

Marilyn Hacker is the author of eight books, most recently *Winter Numbers* and *Selected Poems 1965–1990*. She received the National Book Award for *Presentation Piece* and Lambda Literary Awards for *Going Back to the River* and *Winter Numbers*.

Julie Hall received her M.F.A. in creative writing from Goddard College.

Jan Hardy is the editor and publisher of the anthologies *Wanting Women: An Anthology of Erotic Lesbian Poetry*; and *Sister/Stranger: Lesbians Loving Across the Lines*. Her writing has been published in the anthology *The Poetry of Sex* and in the journals *Calyx*, *Hurricane Alice*, and *Sinister Wisdom*.

Doris L. Harris is the author of a poetry collection, *Refreshments*. She is the recipient of an Astraea Emerging Lesbian

Writers Fund Award for Poetry and the Nikki Giovanni Poetry Award.

Mary Diane Hausman is the author of the poetry collection *A Born-Again Wife's First Lesbian Kiss*. Her writing has been published in the anthologies *Out of the Dark* and *Sage Within* and in the journals *The New Press Literary Quarterly*, *Webster's Review*, and *Pearl*.

Eloise Klein Healy is the author of the poetry collections *Building Some Changes*, *A Packet Beating Like a Heart*, *Ordinary Wisdom*, and *Artemis in Echo Park* (Lambda Literary Award Finalist). She received the Grand Prize in the Los Angeles Poetry Festival Competition in 1992, and is the Associate Editor of *The Lesbian Review of Books*.

Chaia Heller is the author of *Ecofeminism and the Politics of Desire*. Her writing has appeared in the anthologies *Lesbian Culture* and *Women's Glibber* and in the journals *Calyx* and *Sojourner*.

Marcie Hershman is the author of two novels: *Tales of the Master Race* and *Safe in America*. Her writing has also been published in *The New York Times*, *The Boston Globe*, *Ms.*, and *Bay Windows*.

Karen Jastermsky received an M.F.A. in Creative Writing from Vermont College. Her poetry has been published in the journals *Pebbles*, *The Evergreen Chronicles*, and *Poems and Plays*. She was the 1993 cowinner of the Fourth Annual Chapbook Award sponsored by *Embers*.

Terri L. Jewell is the author of a poetry collection *Succulent Heretic* and the editor of *The Black Woman's Gumbo Ya-Ya:*

Quotations by Black Women. Her writing has been published in the anthologies *When I Am An Old Woman I Shall Wear Purple*; *Serious Pleasure*; *The Poetry of Sex*; and *Piece of My Heart: A Lesbian of Colour Anthology*, and in the journals *African American Review*, *The American Voice*, *Sing Heavenly Muse!*, and *The Bloomsbury Review*. She died in 1995.

Louise Karch has had her writing published in the anthology *Loving in Fear* and in the journals *Xtra Magazine*, *Canadian Woman Studies*, and *Harvard Women's Law Review*. In 1995 she received the Marguerite R. Dow Canadian Heritage Award for Writing.

Willyce Kim is the author of three books of poetry: *Curtains of Light*, *Eating Artichokes*, and *Under the Rolling Sky*, and two books of fiction: *Dancer Dawkins and the California Kid* and *Dead Heat*. Her writing has been published in the anthologies *Amazon Poetry*; *Afterglow*; *Asian American Poetry*; and *Women on Women* and in the journals *Ikon*, *Sinister Wisdom*, and *Rainbow Snake*.

Irena Klepfisz is the author of *A Few Words in the Mother Tongue: Poems Selected and New (1971–1990)*, and *Dreams of an Insomniac: Jewish Feminist Essays, Speeches, and Diatribes*. She also coedited the books *A Tribe of Dina: A Jewish Woman's Anthology* and *A Jewish Woman's Call for Peace: A Handbook for Jewish Women on the Israeli/Palestinian Conflict*.

Jacqueline Lapidus is the author of the poetry collections *Yantras of Womanlove* (with photographs by Tee Corinne), *Ready to Survive*, *Starting Over*, and *Ultimate Conspiracy*. Her writing has been published in the journals *Conditions*,

Heresies, *Sojourner*, and *Sinister Wisdom* and in the anthologies *Amazon Poetry*; *Lesbian Poetry*; and *Sarah's Daughters Sing: A Sampler of Poems by Jewish Women.*

Joan Larkin is the author of two poetry collections: *Housework* and *A Long Sound*, and the coeditor of the anthologies *Amazon Poetry*; *Lesbian Poetry*; and *Gay and Lesbian Poetry in Our Time*. She teaches in the Goddard M.F.A. program in Creative Writing.

Heather Lee has had her writing published in the anthology *The Femme Mystique* and in the journal *Common Lives/Lesbian Lives*.

Denise Nico Leto coedited the anthology *il viaggio delle donne: Italian American Women Reach Shore*. Her writing has been published in the anthology *Unsettling America: An Anthology of Contemporary Multicultural Poetry* and in the journals *Voices in Italian Americana*, *Jejune*, *Paterson Literary Review*, and *Writing For Our Lives*.

Emily Lloyd is a free-lance journalist for lesbian and feminist publications. "At the Michigan Womyn's Music Festival, 1994," is her first published poem.

Audre Lorde is the author of the poetry collections *The Black Unicorn*; *Undersong: Chosen Poems Old and New*; *Our Dead Behind Us*; and *The Marvelous Arithmetics of Distance: Poems 1987–1992*. Her prose titles include *Sister Outsider: Essays and Speeches*; *A Burst of Light: Essays*; *The Cancer Journals*; and *Zami: A New Spelling of My Name: A Biomythography*. Her literary awards include a National Endowment for the

Arts Fellowship, National Book Award Finalist, Before Columbus Foundation American Book Award, the Bill Whitehead Award for Lifetime Achievment, and New York State Poet Laureate. Audre Lorde died in 1992.

Bia Lowe is the author of a book of essays *Wild Ride: Earthquakes, Sneezes and Other Thrills*. Her writing has been published in the anthologies *Sister and Brother: Lesbians and Gay Men Write About Their Lives Together*; *Indivisible: New Short Fiction by West Coast Gay and Lesbian Writers*; and *Blood Whispers: L.A. Writers on AIDS* and in the journals *The Kenyon Review* and *The Beloit Poetry Journal*.

Victoria Lena Manyarrows received an Astraea Emerging Lesbian Writers Fund Award for Poetry in 1994. Her writing has been published in the anthologies *Skin Deep: Women Writing on Color*; *Culture and Identity*; *Without Discovery: A Native Response to Columbus*; and *Piece of My Heart: A Lesbian of Colour Anthology* and in the journals *Indigenous Woman*, *Calyx*, *Hurricane Alice*, and *New Virginia Review*. She is a member of the Native American Writers and Storytellers and the Native Writers Circle of the Americas.

Lynn Martin is the author of a poetry collection, *Visible Signs of Defiance*. Her poetry has been published in the journals *Earth's Daughters*, *Sinister Wisdom*, *Frontiers*, and *Metis*. She received an M.F.A. in Creative Writing from Vermont College.

Ann McBreen is a psychotherapist. "My Old Lover" is her first published poem.

Judith McDaniel is the author of a collection of poetry *November Woman*; two essay and poetry collections: *Metamorphosis: Reflections on Recovery* and *Sanctuary*; two novels: *Winter Passage* and *Just Say Yes*; and the nonfiction book *A Lesbian Couples Guide*.

Christian McEwen is the editor of *Naming the Waves: Contemporary Lesbian Poetry* and coeditor of *Out the Other Side: Contemporary Lesbian Writing*. Her poems have appeared in the anthologies *Love Poems by Women* and *Poems for Peace*. Her literary awards include a Lambda Literary Award and a Fulbright Scholarship.

Mary Ann McFadden is the author of a poetry collection *Eye of the Blackbird*, which was chosen for the Writer's Voice First Book Reading Award. Her poems have appeared in the journals *The American Voice*, *Southern Poetry Review*, and *Mestrel*. She teaches at Brooklyn College.

Susan V. McGovern is the director of a Home Health Agency. "Sex" is her first published poem.

Jane Miller is the author of several poetry collections, including *August Zero* and *American Odalisque* and the essay collection *Working Time: Essays on Poetry, Culture and Travel*. Her literary awards include a Lila Wallace-Reader's Digest Writer's Award, a Guggenheim Fellowship, two National Endowment for the Arts Fellowships, and a grant from the Tucson Arts Council.

Patricia Monaghan is the author of two poetry collections: *Winterburning* and *Seasons of the Witch* and two books of prose: *The Book of Goddesses and Heroines* and *O Mother Sun! A New View of the Cosmic Feminine.*

Honor Moore is the author of a collection of poetry, *Memoir*, and a biography of her grandmother, the painter Margarett Sargent, entitled *The White Blackbird.* Her play *Mourning Pictures* has been produced on Broadway. Her literary awards include fellowships from the National Endowment for the Arts and the Connecticut Commission on the Arts.

Cherríe Moraga is the author of two poetry and essay collections, *Loving in the War Years* and *The Last Generation*, and the coeditor of the anthologies *This Bridge Called My Back: Writings by Radical Women of Color* and *Cuentos: Stories by Latinas.* Her literary awards include the Before Columbus American Book Award, the Fund for New American Plays Award, and the National Endowment for the Arts Theatre Playwrights' Fellowship.

Robin Morgan is the author of the poetry collections *Monster*, *Lady of the Beasts*, and *Upstairs in the Garden: Poems Selected and New 1968–1988*, and the editor of *Sisterhood is Powerful* and *Sisterhood is Global.* Her poetry has been published in the journals *The American Voice*, *The Atlantic*, *Calyx*, *Kalliope*, *Ms.*, *The New England Review*, *off our backs*, *The Women's Review of Books*, and *The Yale Review.*

Bonnie Morris has had her writing published in the anthologies *Out of the Class Closet: Lesbians Speak*; *Sportsdykes*; *Finding Courage*; *New World Hasidism*; and *The Poetry of Sex* and in the journals *Sojourner* and *off our backs.*

Nicola Morris has had her writing published in the anthologies *Word of Mouth*; *Three in One: Women Respond to Cancer*; and *Cancer as a Woman's Issue* and in the journals *Sinister Wisdom* and *The Journal of Feminist Studies and Religion*. She teaches in the M.F.A. in Creative Writing program at Goddard College.

Thérèse Murdza has had her writing published in the journals *Pearl* and *The Evergreen Chronicles*.

Eileen Myles is the author of the poetry collections *Not Me* and *Sappho's Boat* and the short story collection *Chelsea Girls*, which was a Lambda Literary Award Finalist. Her poetry has been published in the anthology *Poets for Life* and in the journals *The World*, *The Little Magazine*, *The Baltimore Sun Magazine*, *Paris Review*, *Ploughshares*, and *The Brooklyn Review*.

Lesléa Newman is the author of two poetry collections: *Love Me Like You Mean It* and *Sweet Dark Places*; the novel *In Every Laugh a Tear*; the short story collections *A Letter To Harvey Milk* and *Every Woman's Dream*; the children's book *Heather Has Two Mommies*; and the anthology *The Femme Mystique*. Three of her books were Lambda Literary Award Finalists and she is the recipient of a Massachusetts Artists Foundation Fellowship in Poetry.

Barbara Noda is the author of the poetry collection *Strawberries* and the play *Aw Shucks! (Shikata Ga Nai)*, produced in 1981 by the Asian American Theater Company. Her writing has been published in the anthologies *Lesbian Po-*

etry, *Lesbian Fiction*; *This Bridge Called My Back: Writings By Radical Women of Color*, and *The Poetry of Sex*.

Karen Lee Osborne is the author of two novels: *Hawkwings* and *Carlyle Simpson*, which won First Prize from the Friends of American Writers and the Chicago Foundation for Literature Award. She is the editor of *The Country of Herself: Short Fiction by Chicago Women* and coeditor of *Reclaiming the Heartland*, a lesbian and gay anthology.

Sheila J. Packa has had her writing published in the journals *Ploughshares*, *Earth's Daughters*, *Sinister Wisdom*, *Sing Heavenly Muse!*, *Hurricane Alice*, *Rag Mag*, and *North Coast Review*. She received an M.F.A. in Creative Writing from Goddard College and has won a Loft McKnight Award for Poetry and a Loft Mentor Award for Poetry.

H. Emilia Paredes received an Astraea Emerging Lesbian Writers Fund Award for Poetry in 1993. Her writing has been published in the anthologies *New Chicana/Chicano Writing Vol. 2*; *Currents from the Dancing River: Contemporary Latino Writing*; and *The Key to Everything: Classic Lesbian Love Poems*.

Pat Parker is the author of the poetry collections *Child of Myself*, *Pit Stop*, *Womanslaughter*, *Movement in Black*, and *Jonestown and Other Madness*. Her writing has been published in the anthologies *Home Girls: A Black Feminist Anthology*; *This Bridge Called My Back: Writings by Radical Women of Color*; *Lesbian Poetry*; and *Amazon Poetry*. Pat Parker died in 1989.

Gerry Gomez Pearlberg is the editor of *The Key To Everything: Classic Lesbian Love Poems*. Her writing has been published in the anthologies *Sister and Brother: Lesbians and Gay Men Write About Their Lives Together*; *The Femme Mystique*; and *Women on Women 3*.

Meredith Pond received an M.F.A. in Creative Writing from American University. Her writing has been published in the anthology *From Wedded Wife to Lesbian Life*. She received the *Folio Literary Journal's* Award for Poetry in 1993.

Deidre Pope has had her work published in the journals *Spoon River Poetry Review*, *Northwest Review*, *Primavera*, *Beloit Poetry Journal*, *Sojourner*, and *Seattle Review*. Her literary awards include a Pushcart Prize nomination and Second Prize in the Corson Bishop Prize in Poetry from Cornell University.

Carol Potter is the author of two poetry collections: *Before We Were Born* and *Upside Down in the Dark*. Her poetry has been published in the journals *The American Poetry Review*, *Field*, *Sojourner*, *The Women's Review of Books*, and *The Iowa Review*. She won the *New Letters* Award for Poetry in 1990.

Amanda Powell has had her writing published in the journals *Ploughshares*, *Sinister Wisdom*, and *The Women's Review of Books*. Her literary awards include fellowships from the Massachusetts Artists Foundation, the National Endowment for the Humanities, and the Oregon Arts Commission.

Mary Clare Powell is the author of *The Widow* and *This Way Daybreak Comes: Women's Values and the Future*. She is on the faculty at Lesley College.

Minnie Bruce Pratt is the author of the poetry collection *Crime Against Nature*, which was chosen as the 1989 Lamont Poetry Selection by the Academy of American Poets, nominated for a Pulitzer Prize, and received the American Library Association's Gay and Lesbian Book Award for Literature. Her other titles include a book of poetry, *We Say We Love Each Other*; a book of essays, *Rebellion: Essays 1980–1991*; and a book of prose, *S/he*.

Liz Queeney is a social worker. "Kissing Coco" is her first publication in an anthology.

Shelly Rafferty has had her writing published in the anthologies *Lesbian Love Stories*; *Lesbian Bedtime Stories Vol. I*; *Word of Mouth*; and *Quickies: Lesbian Short-Shorts*, and in the journals *The Evergreen Chronicles*, *Common Lives/Lesbian Lives*, and *The Lesbian Review of Books*.

Berta Ramirez has had her writing published in the journal *esto no tiene nombre* and the anthology *Body of Love*. She is a photographer as well as a writer.

Margaret Randell is the author of over two dozen books, including the poetry collections *A Poetry of Resistance*, *The Coming Home Poems*, *This is About Incest*, *Memory Says Yes*, and *Dancing With the Doe*. Her writing has been published in the journals *The Nation*, *Chelsea Review*, *The Village Voice*, *Heresies*, *New Directions*, *Ms.*, *The American Book Review*, and *The American Poetry Review*.

Adrienne Rich is the author of numerous books of poetry, including *Diving into the Wreck*, *The Dream of a Common*

Language, *A Wild Patience Has Taken Me This Far*, *Time's Power*, *An Atlas of the Difficult World*, and *The Fact of a Doorframe: Poems Selected and New: 1950–1984*. Her literary awards include two Guggenheim Fellowships, a grant from the National Institute of Arts and Letters, and a fellowship from the MacArthur Foundation of Chicago.

Margaret Robison is the author of two books of poetry: *The Naked Bear* and *Red Creek*. Her writing has been published in the journals *Sojourner*, *Disability Rag*, *Sinister Wisdom*, and *Yankee Magazine*.

Victoria Alegría Rosales has had her writing published in the anthologies *Skin Deep: Women Writing on Color, Culture and Identity* and *The Sexuality of Latinas Anthology* and in the journals *The Poetry Conspiracy*, *The San Francisco Bay Guardian*, *Sinister Wisdom*, and *Odessa Poetry Review*.

Muriel Rukeyser is the author of fifteen collections of poetry, including *The Gates*, *Body of Waking*, *The Green Wave*, *A Turning Wind*, *U.S. 1*, and *The Collected Poems of Muriel Rukeyser*. Her first poetry collection, *Theory of Flight*, won the Yale Younger Poets Award in 1935. Muriel Rukeyser died in 1980.

Kate Rushin is the author of a collection of poetry *The Black Back-ups*. Her writing has been published in the anthologies *Home Girls: A Black Feminist Anthology; This Bridge Called My Back: Writings by Radical Women of Color*, and *An Ear To the Ground: Contemporary American Poetry* and in the journals *Conditions*, *Dark Horse*, *Sojourner*, and *The Women's Review of Books*.

Sue Russell has had her writing published in the anthology *Sister/Stranger: Lesbians Loving Across the Lines* and in the journals *The Kenyon Review, Lambda Book Report, Poets & Writers*, and *The Women's Review of Books*.

Ruth L. Schwartz is the author of the collection of poetry *Accordian Breathing and Dancing*, which won the 1994 Associated Writing Program Contest. Her literary awards include an Astraea Emerging Lesbian Writers Fund Award for Poetry and a fellowship from the National Endowment for the Arts.

Maureen Seaton is the author of two collections of poetry: *The Sea Among the Cupboards* and *Fear of Subways*. Her poems have been published in the journals *The Kenyon Review, The Paris Review*, and *The New England Review* and she has received fellowships from the National Endowment for the Arts and the Illinois Arts Council.

Anita Skeen is the author of the poetry collection *Each Hand A Map*. Her poetry has been published in the anthologies *I Hear My Sisters Saying* and *Confluence: Contemporary Kansas Writers* and in the journals *Kansas Quarterly, New Letters, Nimrod, 13th Moon*, and *Yellow Silk*.

Margaret Sloan-Hunter is the author of the poetry collection *Black and Lavender*. Her writing has been published in *The New York Times, Chicago Tribune, Ms. Magazine*, and *The Civil Rights Digest*. She is one of the founding editors of *Ms. Magazine*, as well as the first Chairwoman of the National Black Feminist Organization, founded in 1973.

Linda Smukler is the author of the poetry collection *Normal Sex*, which was a Lambda Literary Award Finalist. Her poems have been published in the anthologies *Gay and Lesbian Poetry in Our Time*; *Love's Shadow*; and *Naming the Waves: Contemporary Lesbian Poetry* and in the journals *The Kenyon Review*, *The American Voice*, *New England Review/Bread Loaf Quarterly*, *Sinister Wisdom*, and *13th Moon*. She is the recipient of an Astraea Emerging Lesbian Writers Fund Award for Poetry.

Indigo Som has had her writing published in the anthologies *Piece of My Heart: A Lesbian of Colour Anthology* and *The Very Inside: An Anthology of Writing by Asian and Pacific Islander Lesbians and Bisexual Women*.

June Blue Spruce is the author of the poetry collection *clear cut*. Her writing has been published in the journals *Northwest Passage* and *off our backs*.

Susan Stinson is the author of two novels, *Fat Girl Dances With Rocks* and *Martha Moody*, and a collection of poetry and stories *Belly Songs: In Celebration of Fat Women*.

Sharon Stricker has had her work published in the anthology *In A Different Light: An Anthology of Lesbian Writers* and the journals *Heresies* and *Writing for Our Lives*. She has received literary awards from the California Arts Council, the National Endowment for the Arts and the Ms. Foundation.

May Swenson is the author of ten volumes of poems, including *Another Animal*, *In Other Words*, *New and Selected Things Taking Place*, and *The Love Poems of May Swenson*. Her writing has been published in the journals *American Poetry*

Review, *Atlantic Monthly*, *Harper's*, *The Nation*, *The New Yorker*, and *Saturday Review*. Her literary awards include the Bollingen Prize in Poetry and a MacArthur Foundation fellowship. May Swenson died in 1989.

Sheila Ortiz Taylor is the author of the poetry collection *Slow Dancing at Miss Polly's*. She teaches Creative Writing and Women's Studies at Florida State University in Tallahassee.

Kitty Tsui is the author of the poetry collection *The Words of a Woman Who Breathes Fire*. Her poetry has been published in the anthologies *Lesbian Erotics*; *Pearls of Passion*; *Chloe Plus Olivia*; and *The Very Inside: An Anthology of Writing by Asian and Pacific Islander Lesbians and Bisexual Women*.

Kim Vaeth is the author of the poetry collection *Her Yes*. Her poetry has been published in the journals *The Women's Review of Books*, *Ploughshares*, *The American Voice*, *The Kenyon Review*, and *13th Moon*. Her literary awards include a Massachusetts Artists Foundation Fellowship, a Pushcart Prize nomination, and a Dewar's Artists' Profiles Award.

Sarah Van Arsdale is the author of the novel *Toward Amnesia*. Her writing has been published in the journals *Passages North*, *The G.W. Review*, *Tributary*, and *Hellas: The Journal of Radical Neo-Classicism*. She received an M.F.A. in Creative Writing from Vermont College.

Diane Vance has had her work published in the journal *Southwestern Review*.

Chocolate Waters is the author of three collections of poetry: *To the man reporter from the Denver Post*, *Take Me Like a*

Photograph, and *Charting New Waters*. She is the recipient of a Barbara Deming Memorial Fund Grant and a New York Foundation for the Arts poetry grant.

Jessica Weissman is a computer programmer and multimedia developer. "Amish Country" is her first published poem.

Aryn A. Whitewolf has had her writing published in the journals *The Irish Wolfhound Quarterly* and *The "L" Word*.

Brooke Wiese has had her poems published in the journals *Anathema Review*, *Atlanta Review*, *The Laurel Review*, *The Ledge*, and *Onion River Review*. Her literary awards include two Pushcart Prize nominations.

Julia Willis is the author of two books of prose: *Who Wears the Tux?* and *We Oughta Be in Pictures*, which was a Lambda Literary Award Finalist. Her literary awards include fellowships from the Massachusetts Artists Foundation and the Edward Albee Foundation.

Judith K. Witherow has had her writing published in the journals *The Wayah Review*, *Sinister Wisdom*, *Quest: A Feminist Quarterly*, *Sojourner*, and *off our backs*. In 1994 she won the first annual Audre Lorde Memorial Prose Contest.

Terry Wolverton is the author of the poetry collection *Black Slip*, which was a Lambda Literary Award Finalist. She is the editor of the anthologies *Indivisible: New Short Fiction by West Coat Gay and Lesbian Writers*; *Blood Whispers: L.A. Writers on AIDS*; and *Hers*.

Merle Woo has had her writing published in *This Bridge Called My Back: Writings by Radical Women of Color*, *The*

Very Inside: An Anthology of Writing by Asian and Pacific Islander Lesbians and Bisexual Women; and *Forbidden Stitch: An Asian American Women's Anthology.*

Kim Yaged received the Hopwood Award and the Atanas Ilitch Award for her play *Roomies*. Her writing has been published in the journals *The Michigan Daily*, *Honi Soit*, *Union Recorder*, and *Womyn's Press*.

Shay Youngblood is the author of the short story collection *The Big Mama Stories* and the plays *Shakin' the Mess Outta Misery*, *Talking Bones*, *Square Blues*, and *Hotel De Dream*. Her literary awards include an Edward Albee Award, an Astraea Emerging Lesbian Writers Fund Award for Fiction, a Lorraine Hansberry Playwriting Award, and an NAACP Playwriting Award.

Yvonne Zipter is the author of the poetry collection *The Patience of Metal*, which was a runner-up for the Poetry Society of America's Melville Cane Award and a Lambda Literary Award Finalist. She is also the author of a book of humor, *Ransacking the Closet*, and a book of nonfiction, *Diamonds Are a Dyke's Best Friend.*

Grateful acknowledgment is made for permission to reprint the following poems:

"Looking Back" and "Pretty Dark in the Morning" Copyright © 1995 by Donna Allegra. Reprinted by permission of the author.

"He Na Tye Woman" Copyright © 1982 by Paula Gunn Allen and the Board of Regents of the University of California. Reprinted from *Shadow Country* by Paula Gunn Allen, who gives thanks to the Board of Regents of the University of California, and the American Indian Studies Center, UCLA. Reprinted by permission of the author.

"Reason Enough To Love You" from *The Women Who Hate Me* by Dorothy Allison. Copyright © 1991 by Dorothy Allison. Reprinted by permission of Firebrand Books, Ithaca, NY.

"Honeydew Night" Copyright © 1988 by Paula Amann.

"Cookery" Copyright © 1990 by Paula Amann. Previously published in *Sister/Stranger: Lesbians Loving Across the Lines*, edited by Jan Hardy (Sidewalk Revolution Press, 1993). Reprinted by permission of the author.

"songs towards you" Copyright © 1996 by Ghazala Anwar. Reprinted by permission of the author.

"AT&T" Copyright © 1994 by V.K. Aruna. Previously published in *The Very Inside: An Anthology of Writing by Asian and Pacific Islander Lesbian and Bisexual Women*, edited by Sharon Lim-Hing (Sister Vision Press, Toronto, Canada 1994). Reprinted by permission of the author.

"The Door of Spring" and "The Wind/Door" Copyright © 1996 by Jane Barnes. Reprinted by permission of the author.

"Undertow" Copyright © 1995 by Judith Barrington. Reprinted by permission of the author.

"When We Talked in the Rose Garden" Copyright © 1985 by Judith Barrington, from *Trying To Be An Honest Woman* by Judith Barrington (The Eighth Mountain Press, 1985). Reprinted by permission of the author and The Eighth Mountain Press.

"To Praise" Copyright © 1983 by Ellen Bass. Previously published in *Calyx*, Vol. 8 No. 1, Fall 1983. Reprinted by permission of the author.

"Holding Hands with Janet after the Accident" Copyright © 1992 by Ellen Bass. Reprinted by permission of the author.

"For Janet, at the New Year" Copyright © 1984 by Ellen Bass. Previously published in a different version in *The Feminist Press 1970–1985: A Birthday Book* (The Feminist Press, 1988). Reprinted by permission of the author.

"Fable" from *Giacometti's Dog* by Robin Becker, Copyright © 1990 by Robin Becker. Reprinted by permission of the University of Pittsburgh Press.

"Morning Poem" Copyright © 1982 by Robin Becker from *Back-*

talk by Robin Becker (Alice James Books, 1982). Reprinted by permission of Alice James Books.

"Married Ladies Have Sex in the Bathroom" Copyright © 1992 by Sally Bellerose. Previously published in *The Poetry of Sex*, edited by Tee Corinne (Banned Books, 1992); *Women on Women 2*, edited by Joan Nestle and Naomi Holoch (Plume, June 1993); and *Sex Crimes* by Sally Bellerose, edited by Janet Aalfs, Sally Bellerose, and Susan Stinson, Orogeny Press, 1995. Copyright © 1995 by Sally Bellerose (Orogeny Press, 1995). Reprinted by permission of the author.

"My Next Lover" Copyright © 1991 by Becky Birtha from *The Forbidden Poems* by Becky Birtha (Seal Press, 1991). Reprinted by permission of the publisher.

"Eleven Months" © 1991 Becky Birtha. Previously published in *Friends for Lesbian and Gay Concerns Newsletter*, Issue #57, Spring 1991. Reprinted by permission of the author.

"Personals" and "Burying the Cat" Copyright © 1996 by Margaret Cardea Black. Reprinted by permission of the author.

"Because They Are Mine" Copyright © 1992 by Nancy Boutilier. Reprinted from *According To Her Contours* by Nancy Boutilier with the permission of Black Sparrow Press.

"Sometimes, as a child" from *Beginning with O* by Olga Broumas. Copyright © 1977 by Olga Broumas. Reprinted by permission of Yale University Press.

"She Loves" from *Perpetua* by Olga Broumas. Copyright © 1989 by Olga Broumas. Reprinted by permission of Copper Canyon Press, PO Box 271, Port Townsend, WA 98368.

"Skylight" Copyright © 1990 by Jayne Relaford Brown. Previously published in *Silver-Tongued Sapphistry* edited by Lynne Bush (Silver Tongued Sapphists Press, San Diego, CA 1990). Reprinted by permission of the author.

"As You Fly to Chicago: A Confession" Copyright © 1993 by Jayne Relaford Brown. Previously published in *The Flight of the Eagle/El Vuelo del Aguila: Poetry on the U.S.-Mexican Border* edited by Harry Polkinhorn, Rogelio Reyes, and Gabriel Trujillo Muñoz. (Binational Press/Editorial Binacional, Calexico/Mexicali, 1993). Reprinted by permission of the author.

"Two Songs for Touch" Copyright © 1995 by Jayne Relaford Brown. Reprinted by permission of the author.

"Rondel du Jour" Copyright © 1996 by Melissa Cannon. Reprinted by permission of the author.

"Note to My Lover's Brother" Copyright © 1996 by Lori Cardona. Reprinted by permission of the author.

"Anything" and "To hold me inside out" Copyright © 1996 by Ana Marie Castañon. Reprinted by permission of the author.

"Last Kiss" and "Missing You" Copyright © 1996 by Laura Castellanos del Valle. Reprinted by permission of the author.

"You Ask Me for a Love Name," "Your Fingers Are Still," and "This Is" Copyright © 1993 by Chrystos from *In Her I Am* (Press Gang Publishers, Vancouver, Canada 1993). Reprinted by permission of the author.

"How to Talk to a New Lover about Cerebral Palsy" and "Tremors" Copyright © 1996 by Elizabeth Clare. Reprinted by permission of the author.

"Buttons" from *Experimental Love* by Cheryl Clarke. Copyright © 1993 by Cheryl Clarke. Reprinted by permission of Firebrand Books, Ithaca, NY.

"nothing" from *Living As A Lesbian* by Cheryl Clarke. Copyright © 1986 by Cheryl Clarke. Reprinted by permission of Firebrand Books, Ithaca, NY.

"Two Thieves" Copyright © 1996 by Martha Courtot. Reprinted by permission of the author.

"Special Delivery," "So This Is Love," and "Lover's Wish" Copyright © 1990 by Patricia Donegan from *Without Warning* (Parallax Press, Berkeley, CA 1990). Reprinted by permission of Parallax Press, Berkeley, California.

"The Butch Speaks" and "Dream Lover" Copyright © 1996 by Amy Edgington. Reprinted by permission of the author.

"Island Dream" Copyright © 1994 by Ana Bantigue Fajardo. Previously published in *The Very Inside: An Anthology of Writing by Asian and Pacific Islander Lesbian and Bisexual Women*, edited by Sharon Lim-Hing (Sister Vision Press, 1994). Reprinted by permission of the author.

"First of the Motorcycle Poems" Copyright © 1988 by Lori Faulkner. "Second of the Motorcycle Poems" Copyright © 1996 by Lori Faulkner. Reprinted by permission of the author.

"We Always Were" Copyright © 1992 by Folisade from *Quicksand! African American Lesbian Erotica* by Folisade (Black Angels Press, 1992). Previously published in *Sisterfire: Black Womanist Fiction and Poetry*, edited by Charlotte Watson Sherman (HarperPerennial, 1994). Reprinted by permission of the author.

"Sonnet" Copyright © 1993 by Beatrix Gates. Previously published in *The Women's Review of Books*, 1993. Reprinted by permission of the author.

"Main line" Copyright © 1996 by Shahara Lauren Godfrey. Reprinted by permission of the author.

"Poem With an Attitude" Copyright © 1994 by Lynn Goldfarb. Reprinted by permission of the author.

"My Chakabuku Mama" Copyright © 1986 by Jewelle Gomez from *Flamingoes and Bears* by Jewelle Gomez (Grace Publications, 1986). Reprinted by permission of the author.

"Keystone" Copyright © 1994 by Jewelle Gomez. Reprinted by permission of the author.

"Who I Am" and "Trouble" Copyright © 1988 by Melinda Goodman from *Middle Sister* by Melinda Goodman (MSG Press, 1988). Reprinted by permission of the author.

"Sweet Dreams," "My Sweet Cynic," and "Visit Me" Copyright © 1996 by Adele Gorelick. Reprinted by permission of the author.

"My Crush on the Yakima Woman" from *Beneath My Heart* by Janice Gould. Copyright © 1990 by Janice Gould. Reprinted by permission of Firebrand Books, Ithaca, NY.

"Companion" Copyright © 1991 by Janice Gould. Previously published in *Berkeley Poetry Review 25 (1991–1992)* and *The Poetry of Sex*, edited by Tee Corinne (Banned Books, 1992). Reprinted by permission of the author.

"Kissing at the Counter" and "Valentine" Copyright © 1995 by Tzivia Gover. Reprinted by permission of the author.

"a funeral: plainsong from a younger woman to an older woman" Copyright © 1974 by Judy Grahn from *The Work of a Common Woman* by Judy Grahn (originally published by Diana Press, 1977). Reprinted by permission of the author.

"Differences" Copyright © 1982 by Pamela Gray. Previously published in *Love's Shadow*, edited by Amber Coverdale Sumrall (The Crossing Press, 1993). Reprinted by permission of the author.

"a hollywood ending" Copyright © 1993 by Pamela Gray. Previously published in *Common Lives/Lesbian Lives*, Number 50, Spring 1994. Reprinted by permission of the author.

"First, I want to make you come in my hand" and "You, little one, are just the kind of boy" Copyright © 1986 by Marilyn Hacker from *Love, Death and the Changing of the Seasons*, originally published by Arbor House/William Morrow, 1986, reissued by W.W. Norton & Company, Inc., 1995. Reprinted by permission of the author.

"Finding the Deer" Copyright © 1993 by Julie Hall. Reprinted by permission of the author.

"First Love" Copyright © 1996 by Julie Hall. Reprinted by permission of the author.

"The Moment Before Our Lips Came Together" and "wild honey" Copyright © 1987 by Jan Hardy. Reprinted by permission of the author.

"Quality Time" Copyright © 1993 by Doris L. Harris from *Refreshments*, by Doris L. Harris (published by Doris L. Harris). Reprinted by permission of the author.

"Climb Inside of Me" Copyright © 1996 by Doris L. Harris. Reprinted by permission of the author.

"A Born-Again Wife's First Lesbian Kiss" Copyright © 1995 by Mary Diane Hausman. Previously published in *Pearl*, Spring issue, March 1996. Reprinted by permission of the author.

"Six Years Ten Months" Copyright © 1995 by Mary Diane Hausman. Reprinted by permission of the author.

"My Love Wants to Park" Copyright © 1981 by Eloise Klein Healy from *A Packet Beating Like a Heart* (Books of a Feather, 1981). Reprinted by permission of the author.

"In Praise of Breasts" Copyright © 1996 by Eloise Klein Healy. Reprinted by permission of the author.

"Syllables," "Plum Poem," and "After Language" Copyright © 1995 by Chaia Heller. Reprinted by permission of the author.

"Making Love to Alice" Copyright © 1975 by M.F. Hershman. Reprinted by permission of Marcie Hershman.

"The Ride" and "Faye Dunaway at the Emmys, 1994" Copyright © 1996 by Karen Jastermsky. Reprinted by permission of the author.

"Only Dream" Copyright © 1994 by Terri L. Jewell. Reprinted by permission of the author.

"Unbridled" Copyright © 1996 by Louise Karch. Reprinted by permission of the author.

"HomeComing" Copyright © 1984 by Willyce Kim. Previously published in *IKON*, Second Series #3, Spring/Summer 1984. Reprinted by permission of the author.

"Landscaping" Copyright © 1984 by Willyce Kim. Reprinted by permission of the author.

"Of love and guns in the wild wild West" Copyright © 1988 by Willyce Kim. Reprinted by permission of the author.

"it was good" from *A Few Words in the Mother Tongue: Poems Selected and New 1971–1990* by Irena Klepfisz. Copyright © 1975 by Irena Klepfisz. Reprinted by permission of the author and The Eighth Mountain Press.

"On your back you look like a scaled-down version" and "You look divine in drag: though I won't wear" Copyright © 1985 by Jacqueline Lapidus. Reprinted by permission of the author.

"Some Unsaid Things" Copyright © 1975 by Joan Larkin from

Housework by Joan Larkin (Out & Out Books, 1975). Reprinted by permission of the author.

"Breathing You In" Copyright © 1993 by Joan Larkin. Previously published in *Hanging Loose 63* (Hanging Loose Press, 1993). Reprinted by permission of the author.

"right here, right now" Copyright © 1996 by Heather Lee. Reprinted by permission of the author.

"What I Think of When You're Gone" Copyright © 1996 by Denise Nico Leto. Reprinted by permission of the author.

"At the Michigan Womyn's Music Festival, 1994" Copyright © 1995 by Emily Lloyd. Reprinted by permission of the author.

"Woman" is reprinted from *The Black Unicorn* by Audre Lorde with the permission of W. W. Norton & Company, Inc. Copyright © 1978 by Audre Lorde.

"Love Poem" is reprinted from *Undersong: Chosen Poems Old and New* by Audre Lorde with the permission of W. W. Norton & Company, Inc. Copyright © 1992 by Audre Lorde.

"If It Happens During the Day" Copyright © 1989 by Bia Lowe. Previously published in *In A Different Light: An Anthology of Lesbian Writers*, edited by Carolyn Weathers and Jenny Wrenn (Clothespin Fever Press, 1989). Reprinted by permission of the author.

"Take Me With You Now" Copyright © 1995 by Victoria Lena Manyarrows from *Songs of the Native Lands* by Victoria Lena Manyarrows (Nopal Press, 1995). Reprinted by permission of the author.

"Touch" Copyright © 1992 by Victoria Lena Manyarrows. Previously published in *ELF: Eclectic Literary Forum*, Vol. 2 No. 2, Summer 1992. Reprinted by permission of the author.

"The haircut" Copyright © 1988 by Lynn Martin. Previously published in an earlier form in *5 A.M.*, Vol. 2 No. 1. Reprinted by permission of the author.

"Rainy day" Copyright © 1996 by Lynn Martin. Reprinted by permission of the author.

"My Old Lover" Copyright © 1996 by Ann McBreen. Reprinted by permission of the author.

"Body of Love I and II" Copyright © 1995 by Judith McDaniel. Reprinted by permission of the author.

"And Sunday Morning" Copyright © 1990 by Christian McEwen. Previously published in *Love Poems by Women*, edited by Wendy Mulford (Ballantine Books, 1990). Reprinted by permission of the author.

"Marriage" Copyright © 1994 by Mary Ann McFadden. Previously published in *The American Voice*, Number 33, Spring 1994. Reprinted by permission of the author.

"Sex" Copyright © 1996 by Susan V. McGovern. Reprinted by permission of the author.

"The Healing Fountains" and "New Body" from *August Zero* Copyright © 1993 by Jane Miller. Reprinted by permission of Copper Canyon Press, PO Box 271, Port Townsend, WA 98368.

"The Goddess Pomona Sings to the Old Woman" and "Diana to Her Maiden" Copyright © 1992 by Patricia Monaghan from *Seasons of the Witch* by Patricia Monaghan (Delphi Press, 1992). Reprinted by permission of the author.

"Shenandoah" Copyright © 1988 by Honor Moore from *Memoir* by Honor Moore (Chicory Blue Press, 1988). Reprinted by permission of the author.

"Loving in the War Years" Copyright © 1983 by Cherríe Moraga from *Loving in the War Years*, by Cherríe Moraga (South End Press, 1983). Reprinted by permission of South End Press.

"If" Copyright © 1993 by Cherríe Moraga from *The Last Generation*, by Cherríe Moraga (South End Press, 1993). Reprinted by permission of South End Press.

"Damn You, Lady" is reprinted from *Upstairs in the Garden: Poems Selected and New 1968–1988* by Robin Morgan, with the permission of W.W. Norton & Company, Inc. Copyright © 1990, 1988, 1982 by Robin Morgan.

"Loving You Has Become a Political Act" Copyright © 1988 by Bonnie Morris. Previously published in *Wanting Women: An Anthology of Erotic Lesbian Poetry*, edited by Jan Hardy (Sidewalk Revolution Press, 1990). Reprinted by permission of the author.

"A Partial Eclipse" Copyright © 1996 by Nicola Morris. Reprinted by permission of the author.

"eating szechuan eggplant" and "in the garden" Copyright © 1993 by Thérèse Murdza. Previously published in earlier versions in *Letters from CAMP Rehoboth*, July 29, 1993. Reprinted by permission of the author.

"I always put my pussy" Copyright © 1990 by Eileen Myles. Previously published in *The Kenyon Review* Vol. XIV, Number 1, Winter 1992. Reprinted by permission of the author.

"Nothing Like It" Copyright © 1991 by Lesléa Newman from *Sweet Dark Places* by Lesléa Newman (HerBooks, 1991). Reprinted by permission of the author.

"Night on the Town" Copyright © 1995 by Lesléa Newman. Previously published in *The Femme Mystique*, edited by Lesléa Newman (Alyson Publications, 1995) and *Tangled Sheets: Stories and*

James Books, 1990). Reprinted by permission of Alice James Books.

"Aubade" Copyright © 1987 by Amanda Powell. Part III in an earlier version was previously published in *Bay Windows*, July 21, 1987. Reprinted by permission of the author.

"Lesbian Menopause" and "Love Poem: To Violet" Copyright © 1996 by Mary Clare Powell. Reprinted by permission of the author.

"To Be Posted on 21st Street, Between Eye and Pennsylvania" Copyright © 1988 by Minnie Bruce Pratt. Reprinted by permission of the author.

"Kissing Coco" Copyright © 1996 by Liz Queeney. Reprinted by permission of the author.

"Positive (Revisited)" Copyright © 1992 by Shelly Rafferty. Previously appeared in a different version under the title "Positive" in *Quickies: Lesbian Short-Shorts*, edited by Irene Zahava (Violet Ink Press, 1992). Reprinted by permission of the author.

"Sweetheart Together" and "Together in the wind" Copyright © 1996 by Berta Ramirez. Reprinted by permission of the author.

"I Am Loving You" Copyright © 1995 by Margaret Randall. Reprinted by permission of the author.

"Love Poem" is reprinted from *Time's Power: Poems: 1985–1988* by Adrienne Rich by permission of the author and W. W. Norton & Company, Inc. Copyright © 1989 by Adrienne Rich.

"Two Days Before My Stroke," "Gold," and "I Opened My Hand" Copyright © 1991 by Margaret R. Robison. Reprinted by permission of the author.

"Your Red, Red Lips" and "Cat's Eyes" Copyright © 1996 by Victoria Alegría Rosales. Reprinted by permission of the author.

"Looking At Each Other" by Muriel Rukeyser, from *A Muriel Rukeyser Reader*, published by W. W. Norton & Company, Inc. New York, NY, 1994. Copyright © 1994 by William L. Rukeyser. Reprinted by permission of William L. Rukeyser.

"A Pacifist Becomes Militant and Declares War" from *The Black Back-ups* by Kate Rushin. Copyright © 1993 by Kate Rushin. Reprinted by permission of Firebrand Books, Ithaca, NY.

"But Is She Jewish?" Copyright © 1993 by Sue Russell. Previously appeared in *Sister/Stranger: Lesbians Loving Across The Lines*, edited by Jan Hardy (Sidewalk Revolution Press, 1993). Reprinted by permission of the author.

"The Last Day of Atonement" Copyright © 1996 by Sue Russell. Reprinted by permission of the author.

"January Vineyards" from *Accordian Breathing and Dancing* Copyright © 1995 by Ruth L. Schwartz. Reprinted by permission of The University of Pittsburgh Press.

"Midnight Supper" Copyright © 1996 by Ruth L. Schwartz. Reprinted by permission of the author.

"The Bed" and "A Poverty of Robins" Copyright © 1991 by Maureen Seaton from *Fear of Subways* by Maureen Seaton (The Eighth Mountain Press, 1991). Reprinted by permission of the author and The Eighth Mountain Press.

"These faded blue" Copyright © 1986 by Anita Skeen from *Each Hand A Map* by Anita Skeen (Naiad Press, 1986). Reprinted by permission of the author and publisher.

"Elizabeth Responds to the Separation" Copyright © 1996 by Anita Skeen. Reprinted by permission of the author.

"Longing" and "Sides" Copyright © 1995 by Margaret Sloan-Hunter from *Black and Lavender* by Margaret Sloan-Hunter

(Talking Circles Press, 1995). Reprinted by permission of the author.

"Mom's Best Friend" from *Normal Sex* by Linda Smukler. Copyright © 1994 by Linda Smukler. Reprinted by permission of Firebrand Books, Ithaca, NY.

"earthquake weather" Copyright © 1990 by Indigo Som. Reprinted by permission of the author.

"the very inside" Copyright © 1993 by Indigo Som. Previously published in *The Very Inside: An Anthology of Writing by Asian and Pacific Islander Lesbian and Bisexual Women*, edited by Sharon Lim-Hing (Sister Vision Press, 1994). Reprinted by permission of the author.

"pregnant sex" Copyright © 1995 by June Blue Spruce. Reprinted by permission of the author.

"The Erotics of Morning" and "Home Tongue" Copyright © 1995 by Susan Stinson. Reprinted by permission of the author.

"Cradlesong" Copyright © 1989 by Sharon Stricker. Previously published in *In A Different Light: An Anthology of Lesbian Writers*, edited by Carolyn Weathers and Jenny Wrenn. Reprinted by permission of the author.

"Mornings Innocent" and "Four-Word Lines" from *The Love Poems of May Swenson.* Copyright © 1991 by The Literary Estate of May Swenson. Reprinted by permission of the Houghton Mifflin Company. All rights reserved.

"Confessions of An Escape Artist" Copyright © 1989 by Sheila Ortiz Taylor from *Slow Dancing at Miss Polly's* by Sheila Ortiz Taylor (Naiad Press, 1989). Reprinted by permission of the author and publisher.

"gloriously" and "dragon lover" Copyright © 1996 by Kitty Tsui. Reprinted by permission of the author.

"The Bath" and "Pencil and Blue Crayon" excerpted from *Her Yes* by Kim Vaeth. Copyright © 1994 by Kim Vaeth. Reprinted by permission of Zoland Books in Cambridge, MA.

"Lullabye" Copyright © 1990 by Sarah Van Arsdale. Reprinted by permission of the author.

"Favorite Words" Copyright © 1996 by Diane Vance. Reprinted by permission of the author.

"First Woman" Copyright © 1977 by Chocolate Waters from *Take Me Like a Photograph* by Chocolate Waters (Eggplant Press, 1977). Reprinted by permission of the author.

"Separation" Copyright © 1980 by Chocolate Waters from *Charting New Waters* by Chocolate Waters (Eggplant Press, 1980). Reprinted by permission of the author.

"Amish Country" Copyright © 1995 by Jessica Weissman. Reprinted by permission of the author.

"Bus Stop Lover" Copyright © 1994 by Aryn A. Whitewolf. Reprinted by permission of the author.

"Jazzed Up" Copyright © 1988 by Brooke Wiese. Previously published in *The Ledge*, Number 18, Summer 1995. Reprinted by permission of the author.

"Suddenly! Your Hand" Copyright © 1996 Brooke Wiese. Reprinted by permission of the author.

"SWEET(S)" Copyright © 1995 by Julia Willis. Reprinted by permission of the author.

"Loaded Dice" Copyright © 1993 by Judith K. Witherow. Reprinted by permission of the author.

About the Editor

LESLÉA NEWMAN is an author and editor whose twenty-seven books include the poetry collections *Still Life with Buddy* and *The Little Butch Book*; the short stories collections *Every Woman's Dream* and *A Letter to Harvey Milk*; the novel *In Every Laugh a Tear*; the children's book *Heather Has Two Mommies*; the anthology *The Femme Mystique*; and the collection of humor *Out of the Closet and Nothing to Wear*. Four of her books have been Lambda Literary Award Finalists and she has been the recipient of Poetry Fellowships from the Massachusetts Artists Foundation and the National Endowment for the Arts. She has recently completed a novel entitled *Jailbait* and a novella and short story collection called *Girls Will Be Girls*.

Lesléa Newman invites you to visit her Web site at http://www.lesleanewman.com.